# Civility Rules!

## A new business approach for boosting results and cutting risks

STEPHEN M. PASKOFF

*Civil Treatment*®, *Civil Treatment for Leaders*®, and *Make it matter. Make it simple. Make it stick.*® are all registered trademarks of ELI, Inc.

ISBN-13: 978-0-692-60157-0

www. eliinc.com

ELI, Inc. / 2675 Paces Ferry Road / Suite 470 / Atlanta, GA / 30339

PH: 800-497-7654 or 770-319-7999

# Dedication

This book is dedicated to my wife, Sharon, and to my children, John Eli and Rebecca Matile. Your courage, strength, and love enrich my life and inspire me.

It is also dedicated to the memory of George H. Kaye, my friend and mentor whose kindness, strength, and commitment to fairness and inclusion lives on in me, his family, and everyone else whose life he so generously and wisely touched.

# Acknowledgments

I want to gratefully acknowledge those who helped me write *Civility Rules!*

Sue Reynard worked with me for more than two years as my editor and collaborator. She organized my writing, simplified it, challenged me, and kept this project moving along in line with my vision. Her skill and wisdom were invaluable. I am fortunate to have had the chance to work with her on this project.

Adrienne Morris helped me organize and set aside necessary blocks of time to work on my manuscript. She compiled and maintained the book's many drafts and arranged interviews with those identified in the book.

Amy Gardner designed the cover of this book. She and Jennifer Hershiser also gave me helpful advice on graphic elements and illustrations.

I am fortunate to work with a talented, intelligent, and passionate group of colleagues at ELI. They gave me inspiration through their daily work experiences, insights, and how they work with one another and our clients.

Vaughan Cooper, Ray Amelio and Kay Plantes reviewed this book at various stages of writing. Their experience, wisdom, and candid feedback kept me focused and helped steer me forward.

Stan Wilson, senior partner, and Sean Libby, associate, from Elarbee, Thompson, Sapp & Wilson, reviewed legal authorities for accuracy. I also thank my former colleagues at the firm for their mentorship and collegiality and the opportunity they afforded me.

I learned a lot from the contributions of individuals who provided case studies utilized in this book. My thanks to Dr. Keith Miller, President, and Wendy Walden, Associate Vice President of Executive Affairs (Greenville Technical College); Lee Hardeman, Senior Vice President, Human Resources (First Citizens Bank); and Philip Weis an accomplished and distinguished senior labor and employment lawyer. My thanks also to others whose organizations are anonymously referenced at their request in this book.

Finally, my thanks to Rebecca Ray for being such a remarkable colleague and friend and graciously agreeing to write the foreword to this book.

# Contents

## Part I: Making Civility a Business Issue

# Part II: Persuasion vs. Communication

# Part III: Make It Work

# Foreword

*By Rebecca Ray*

Many years ago, when I looked for a program to help leaders at my organization understand their significant responsibilities (and resultant legal implications), I attended a program offered by Steve Paskoff's company, ELI, called *Civil Treatment for Managers*. The use of scenarios to help leaders understand the challenges and pitfalls as well as to offer insights was fresh and engaging; as participants, we were drawn into discussions that transcended case law and brought us face to face with the concept of a respectful workplace created by a leader who "gets it" rather than one driven by the law. I was hooked. I brought that program, and parallel programs for employees as well as follow-on programs, to every company I have had the privilege to serve. I continued to deliver the program long after I had largely moved out of the training classroom, as I enjoyed watching the transformation of participants; if I am honest, it kept me grounded too.

Now I serve at The Conference Board, one of the world's most respected business membership and research associations working in the public interest. For 100 years, our mission has been unique: to provide the world's leading organizations with the practical knowledge they need to improve their performance and better serve society. I have the rare privilege of seeing some of the world's best companies as they work to create the organizational cultures they believe will attract and retain the best talent, create ethical leaders, foster engagement and innovation, deliver superior value for customers and clients, and achieve a competitive advantage in the marketplace.

Over the years, Steve's friendship and advice have been invaluable, from helping me shape custom programs and create new ones for the companies I worked for, to my personal career decisions. He is one of those rare people who live the words and lead the work in ways that are inextricably linked to their core beliefs ... who believes that leaders can change the lives of others, who then change the organizations they work for, the communities they live in, and the people they love.

In a world where culture matters more than strategy, where a leader's integrity matters more than his or her tacit knowledge, and where leaders must understand the critical role they play in developing a work environment where all people are included and treated with respect, *Civility Rules!* provides the blueprint for leaders to guide the teams they lead to become the teams to which they aspire. It will serve as a guide for helping leaders master what is perhaps the most critical skill they will ever need to develop: lifting people to their potential by creating an environment where that is possible ... a respectful workplace.

*Rebecca Ray*
*Executive Vice President, Knowledge Organization and*
*Human Capital Practice Lead*
*The Conference Board*
*New York, NY*

# Introduction

**I**'m a lawyer by profession. So it may come as something of a surprise that nowadays I spend more of my time talking with business leaders about *civility* than just *legality*. Why the switch? Here's the background:

I started out my career as an investigator and trial attorney at the Equal Employment Opportunity Commission (EEOC) and later became a partner at a management firm that advised and defended corporate clients. Very early on, I began to realize that while my clients wanted to prevent illegal behaviors that could lead to lawsuits, many weren't as concerned about other behaviors that didn't cross the illegal threshold. They'd tolerate or ignore borderline racial, sexual, or age-based remarks or jokes, physical contact taken just a bit too far, or unprofessionalism—as long as the behavior wasn't so extreme as to put them at risk for a lawsuit. Behaviors that were rude, demeaning, or divisive weren't even on the radar screen because they didn't tread on specific legal protections.

My own mentors had taught me to evaluate cases from the standpoint of business impact, and the ignored behaviors seemed unacceptable in a business sense though they were not illegal. The technically legal behaviors were impeding productivity and efficiency, damaging morale and brand image, harming recruitment and retention efforts, and sometimes even creating safety hazards for employees, customers, or the public.

I also saw that, left unchecked, legal-but-uncivil behaviors increased the odds that the offenders (or someone else in the organization) would someday cross over into illegal territory. The path from merely disruptive to outright abusive behaviors is a well-traveled route to illegal actions. Often, unprofessional behavior can taint legal proceedings even when the law has not been violated. I still remember very clearly one trial from many years ago where a jury was outraged by the conduct of a human resources manager, which included swearing and throwing furniture. The guilty verdict was eventually reversed on appeal, but clearly the manager's poor behavior influenced the jury—and though the company avoided stiff monetary penalties, it paid a price both in terms of the drain on resources associated with the legal proceedings and the very real negative impact of that manager's behavior.

Because of these experiences, I came to realize that lawsuits are frequently *not* the worst outcome a company can suffer because of an employee's actions (quite a revelation for a practicing lawyer!). As I'll explore more in this book, legal-but-uncivil behaviors impose costs and occasionally grievous business wounds that rival or exceed what is spent on all but the biggest-ticket lawsuits. As that realization grew, my own focus began expanding beyond legality, and that's when I began to talk to business leaders about the need to broaden their focus as well. As leaders, they had a responsibility to make sure their business or organization complied with laws and regulations. But they also had an operational responsibility, not just a compliance responsibility, to pay attention to the legal behaviors that were harming their organization.

My point of view is that leaders can have a much more positive impact on their business results if they devote increased effort to creating a more civil workplace. I use the term **civil treatment** to encompass all behavior-related issues an organization faces—not just how people treat one another but how comfortable they feel contributing, how well they avoid divisive or harmful actions and words, and how willing they are to speak up about problems. In this way, civil treatment and legality are intertwined: a workplace that focuses on civility is one that not only performs well, but is designed to be in compliance with the law.

Unfortunately, behavioral issues are often viewed as a collateral part of business, as a "soft skill" that is too amorphous to understand and control. I want to challenge the notion that managing behavior and emphasizing civil treatment is a "soft skill." What's soft about preventing millions of dollars in damage? Preserving your firm's reputation? Creating an environment where you can get the most out of your human capital investment? Avoiding breaches of compliance? And perhaps even saving lives? What is soft about investing in the greatest area of cost and investment for most organizations—their employees? When leaders learn to treat civility as a business priority, they can achieve very real business results.

My belief is that leaders must look at behavior with a level of seriousness equal to any other operational issue, business priority, or major initiative. I am not suggesting that people be treated as if they were machines or capital improvement projects. To the contrary, I want to place more focus on people and the individual choices they make every day because those choices are what will create (or destroy) an inclusive, professional, diverse, and legal workplace.

## The Behavioral Core of Diverse Issues

Today, most organizations have separate fiefdoms set up around a variety of desired outcomes like operational performance, compliance, ethics, equal employment, discrimination, and values. But underlying all of these issues is the theme of behavior in the workplace—that is, all of these issues are related to employee conduct, and to when and how work gets done (or not) in an organization.

Focusing on the concepts of civility and civil treatment helps organizations develop a unified approach to behavior—one that fosters a more productive work environment and prevents improper behaviors ranging from the subtlest to the most blatantly illegal. The more an organization understands the behavioral core connecting these diverse issues, the more likely it is to reap widespread benefits measured in terms like safety, inclusion, creativity, productivity, compliance, and other business drivers.

Unfortunately, this unified view of behavior is not common in the workplace. As I'll talk about in Chapter 1, organizations are blinded by legal issues and overlook other behavioral problems that can pose even greater long-term threats. Helping leaders understand the need for a broader mindset is why I decided to write this book. What I discuss here is how to manage all these issues in a way that is as simple and clear as possible:

**Part I: Making Civility a Business Issue** presents the foundations of a more civil workplace, including a discussion of the underappreciated costs that uncivil behavior imposes on an organization, the benefits of bringing all behavior issues under a single umbrella, what is different when organizations adopt a civil treatment approach to dealing with behavior, the dangers of looking for quick fixes, and the benefits of creating a more civil workplace.

**Part II: Persuasion vs. Communication** is focused on the type of effort needed to make sustained changes in behavior. Changing behavior doesn't happen easily, so organizations must look at what they have to do to not just provide initial instruction, but also follow up and reinforce lessons about civil treatment.

**Part III: Make It Work** looks at implementation, from preparing leaders to take an active role, to planning a rollout, to maintaining cultural consistency across the organization.

I wrote this book to make the case that a combined civil-plus-legal mindset is important to business leaders and to give examples of the key elements needed to accomplish this transformation. As we travel this path together, I'll also point out a few simple rules of civility—and hopefully convince you of the many ways in which civility rules!

# *Part I*

# Making Civility a Business Issue

# Creating the Best Workplace Possible

**W**hat is the best possible workplace? In my mind, it is a place that produces results and minimizes negative outcomes; a place where people are engaged and risks are minimized. It is a place where inclusion, respect, integrity, and teamwork help generate great results while keeping the organization operating within the spirit, not just the letter, of the law. It is a place where a commitment to being both legal and civil helps prevent, detect, and ultimately limit compliance risk. As I've seen, having the best possible workplace can also literally be a matter of life and death to employees, their teams, and to the public at large.

At the core of a "best workplace possible" is how work gets done through people. To get the best performance from individuals, a leader's goal has to be creating an environment where:

1) Individuals can do their best and contribute as part of a team.

2) Employees do their work without having behaviors that hinder performance.

3) People feel comfortable in the workplace and believe they can speak up about problems, ideas, and suggestions without risk of being harmed or demeaned or retaliated against (what the experts call "psychological safety").

When you look at workplaces where these conditions are not present—where people can't do their best work individually or as part of a team and don't feel like they can speak up—it's not because of the absence of policies, rules, or systems. It's rather that a culture has sprung up that conflicts with the written standards (a subject I'll discuss in more depth later in this book).

The only way to consistently and reliably get the appropriate behaviors you want to see in your organization, and to minimize uncivil and illegal behaviors, is to create a culture that supports and rewards civil treatment behaviors. That culture needs to make it easier rather than harder for every individual—frontline to executive suite—to contribute to their fullest. It needs to be a culture where the individual choices that people make around their behavior are more likely to positively affect those around them. You want values related to professional, civil behavior to be routine, intuitive, and natural; you want breaches to be a rare, unacceptable deviation (not a routine or pervasive problem).

The following chapters:

- Look at the typical mindset that cripples many organizations' ability to foster civil treatment.

- Present a new model that helps executives put behavioral issues in the right context.

- Show what's gained when civility becomes a positive force for change and business performance.

CHAPTER 1

# The Case for Workplace Civility

In the mid-2000s, I got a call from the vice president of human resources at a world-renowned hospital. One of his hospital's surgical units had what are politely called "people issues." The VP wanted to see if I could present a training program my company had developed specifically for physicians and surgeons that focused on traditional discrimination and harassment topics.

The VP told me the department was experiencing high turnover, had problems recruiting and retaining top candidates, and, not coincidentally, had a very high number of internal complaints about two surgeons. Like the other surgeons in this unit, the two causing the problems were highly skilled and came with outstanding academic credentials and training. But the VP feared there could be a discrimination or harassment lawsuit lurking in the wings and wanted the problem solved.

My legal mind checked through the kinds of conduct that typically lead to lawsuits. I asked the VP whether there was a problem with sexual or racial jokes. He said no. I asked if there were comments about appearance, ethnicity, age, religion, or national origin. Again, none.

He told me about emotional outbursts, condescending remarks, occasional screaming, and explosions of insults, temper, and anger.

Sometimes the people who tried to raise an issue or disagree were ignored or were embarrassed by a surgeon's response. From what I heard, it sounded as if the surgeons were behaving unprofessionally but not illegally: I heard nothing that suggested a civil rights violation, much less assault and battery or other common tort claims.

I realized it would not be productive to teach a course on harassment or discrimination if those weren't the key issues. But I couldn't be sure there wasn't more to the story. So a colleague and I got permission to spend several days meeting with physicians, nurses, and allied health professionals in the department.

What I saw and heard during that visit to "Hospital X"[1] reinforced my thinking that concentrating only on legality and ignoring civility can lead to unnecessary risks and limit what an organization can achieve. In fact, it changed my view about how to look at workplace behavior. Here's the story.

## Surgeons Gone Wild

As I had been told, two surgeons in one particular department at Hospital X did *not* appear to engage in conduct that would constitute workplace discrimination. But the environment they created sounded horrendous. One nurse told my colleague and me that she would not work for one surgeon under any circumstances; another told us that when she did work with that surgeon, she worried more about his mood than the condition of the patient! A third said, "If one of us acted the way he does, we wouldn't be here anymore. We'd be sent out for psychiatric counseling."

---

[1]  The organization that is the subject of this case study is not identified by name here or in any other stories in this book or in any of my other writings or presentations.

We also heard comments like:

- *For 12 hours a day, we take care of their patients, and we're disrespected and degraded in front of each other.*

- *We work together like 3-year-olds play together. We work next to each other, but not with each other. … People are minimally cooperative to get the work done, but not collaborative at all.*

- *The surgeon barks, throws knives and clamps, screams, and curses.*

- *By the end of the surgery, you feel like you've had the worst day of your life.*

My colleague and I later spoke with several anesthesiologists in the department. They had medical degrees from similarly prestigious institutions, shared the same general demographics (gender, age, and race) as the surgeons, and were equally well respected in their field. But they weren't treated as peers. They described the surgeons' behavior as "demeaning, derogatory, antagonistic, and selfish." They commented:

- *Some surgeons micromanage and try to control everything. There's no consideration for what you know, your intelligence.*

- *You shouldn't feel like you're in trouble for bringing up a suggestion.*

- *It's not a good culture here. There's more concern over who you're working with than what you'll have to do.*

- *When four out of five people are scared of you, they'll start to make mistakes. They can't concentrate and can't perform their best.*

During surgery these anesthesiologists not only administered anesthesia but also tracked multiple vital signs. (As an example, if respiration or blood pressure changes dramatically, it can be a sign of imminent danger or even risk of death for the patient.) They both told me that there were times when they were working with the two surgeons that they were reluctant to point out a possible hazard. They worried that speaking up could disrupt the surgeon so much that his outbursts could cause more harm to the patient than if they said nothing and just did their best to cope, hoping and assuming the surgeon would eventually recognize the hazard without their having to point it out to him.

The impact was felt beyond the operating room. We also spoke with post-operative team members who worked in recovery. They told us that the surgeons could be dismissive or condescending, making it clear they weren't interested in the feedback or suggestions of the people taking care of their patients. The usual protocol for these nurses was to remain in close contact with attending surgeons, but with these two poorly behaved surgeons, they sometimes hesitated to reach out, concerned that they would just get yelled at. An all-too-frequent course of action for the nurses was to do everything they could for a patient—short of calling the surgeons.

I found the surgeons' behavior troubling and ironic because surgical teams are *teams* for a reason: it takes multiple people with different talents and abilities to complete a surgery successfully. Even the most gifted surgeon needs a skilled team to do the best work for his or her patient. Yet here, the disruptive behavior of the surgeons undermined teamwork.

## As Long as It's Legal ...

Let me ask you one simple question: would you want any of your loved ones to be treated by either of the two surgeons I just described? I haven't found anyone who answers yes once they hear the full story. All of us shudder when we imagine ourselves or a close family member on an operating table while one of these surgeons is in charge. We can hear the thoughts that would run through our head: *Maybe someone on the team sees something of concern but isn't speaking up. ... Maybe someone is losing focus on a key part of their job responsibility because they fear being screamed at. Did that surgeon just humiliate one of the team? How will that person be able to do their job?*

What made little sense then and even less now is the response I got from the VP. I went over my findings with him, expecting him to be just as aghast as I was. He did a quick verbal triage: "It's not race, age, sex, religion, or any of those categories, so I guess we're OK on the discrimination front."

And there the analysis ended, as did my assignment. "No lawsuit" to him apparently meant "no problem," or at least the problem was not serious enough to warrant action when balanced against the reputation of these doctors and, frankly, the revenue that they produced.

This is not a book about surgeons or healthcare; the same pattern of thinking that pervaded this prestigious institution runs throughout every business sector: banks, manufacturing companies, law and accounting firms, communications companies, government agencies, academic institutions, high-tech startups, and every kind of organization I've ever encountered. Throughout all these organizations, behavior standards are not enforced equally.

I've thought about this situation a lot. I tell the general story frequently (without any specific particulars), and each time audiences react

---

### Things stay the same

The Hospital X incident took place almost a decade ago. As shocking as the outcome is, people get even more aghast when I explain that while such incidents do not happen in every department or every hospital, it remains an industry issue even to this day. While working on this book, I got a call about a prominent surgeon whose behavior was causing problems identical to the ones that Hospital X had with the two poorly behaved surgeons—the same kinds of behaviors, the same kinds of consequences (low morale, high turnover, etc.). *Maybe things really haven't changed much in the past decade,* I thought to myself.

with shock and disbelief. They are just as struck as I was with the impact of the surgeons' behavior not just on the staff but also on patient care.

## Paying Attention to Uncivil Workplace Behavior

The VP was right in one sense: none of the behavior I learned about was overtly illegal or discriminatory in terms of workplace laws. These were highly trained specialists with world-class surgical talent. Yet their behavior falls clearly under what I categorize as **uncivil workplace behavior**. What's that? I include any behavior that:

- Distracts

- Divides

- Marginalizes performance or individuals

- Prevents another person from contributing fully

- Discourages people from speaking up (about problems, risks, ideas, or opportunities)

The uncivil behavior of these surgeons imposed a huge risk to the public and to the institution. On the first phone call, the VP had mentioned specific ways in which the behavior was already costing this hospital—high turnover, dissatisfaction, internal complaints.

That's because uncivil behavior acts like a virus: bad behavior by one person has a negative effect on everyone around them. People who have to listen to complaints will often spread the negative feelings and become disaffected. The spread can reach all corners of a team or organization and also to customers and members of the public (Figure 1).

The viral spread of unrest was evident in Hospital X. Our inquiry identified a wide range of problems, such as a lack of concentration

**Figure 1: The Viral Spread of Uncivil Behavior**

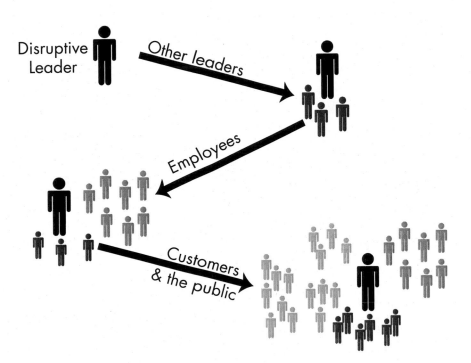

in the OR, residents who would quit the program, the sense that the hospital could no longer get the best medical graduates because of the department's reputation. But these costs (and even the increased *potential* for a lawsuit) didn't appear on the hospital's financial reports as a counterpoint to the revenues generated from the surgeries. So apparently the costs and risks of the surgeons' bad behavior were not taken seriously.

I can't help but wonder if that mentality arises from the belief that aggressive and uncivil behaviors are valuable in some way—that because competition is brutal so must be the workplace environment in order to survive. I had, in fact, asked the two surgeons who were causing problems *why* they screamed, yelled, sometimes threw things, and intimidated others during surgery; they justified their behavior by saying they saw a problem or procedural lapse and were acting "for the good of the patient." (It's the kind of reasoning I've heard a lot, not only from other physicians in similar circumstances but people in diverse professional fields.) Though they may have had legitimate concerns about patient care when they reacted vehemently to perceived errors or lapses on the part of their surgical team, studies have shown that such disruptions may not fix the immediate problem and in fact can create additional problems including botched procedures, complications, and even fatalities. In other words, their behavior may have made any problems worse, not better.

That's unfortunate because uncivil conduct in a hospital is not only boorish and outrageous but as dangerous in its own way as being operated on by an impaired physician, having a procedure done with a defective piece of equipment, or being prescribed a medication with unreported but deadly side effects. The medical literature recognizes that such conduct can lead to surgical complications, incorrect procedures being done, wrong medications being prescribed, and even fatalities (see sidebar). It can drive up costs and drive down outcomes.

---

### Medical costs of unprofessional behavior

A 2011 article in *The New York Times* entitled "Physician Heal Thy Self" explained how unprofessional team behavior—sometimes blatant bullying, sometimes subtler actions such as failing to return calls, unwillingness to answer questions, condescending and sarcastic interactions—can cause complications as well as fatalities. The story suggested that such conduct might be contributing to a rise in avoidable medical errors that, in total, may be causing 200,000 deaths a year.

---

# The Myopia of Illegality

During the time I spent at the hospital, I also met with the CEO (who was himself a renowned physician), the chair of surgery, and the head of the surgery unit, all of whom had direct-line responsibility for the troublesome surgeons. None of them, nor the VP of human resources, seemed compelled to take meaningful action. The attitude of these leaders is what I think of as the **myopia of illegality**: becoming so focused on the legal versus illegal dividing line that you ignore the costs of the legal-but-uncivil behaviors.

In many ways, this myopia is not surprising. In fact, in our litigious society where legal costs, criminal risks, and damages can be crippling, a "legal risk first and only" mindset is understandable. Pick any news source and you'll have an easy time finding stories about the hard dollar costs that illegal behavior has imposed on organizations. Multi-million dollar verdicts are regularly awarded to employees when an organization's leaders fail to take action against harassment or discrimination. Rogue traders[2] and bankers have cost the financial industry billions in recent years. Big dollar stories like these help reinforce the idea that it's *illegal* behavior that brings the big risks and big costs (see sidebar, next page).

Maybe this is why the hospital leaders who assessed the conduct of the surgeons looked at risk in a way that's common in many organizations. While the facts, industry setting, and potential dangers will differ from business to business, if you ask senior executives to assess the risk in a business matter, many will turn first to their lawyers for guidance. They'll seek a legal opinion on topics ranging from employment decisions to work practices, product development, financial transactions, and manufacturing processes.

---

2  Despite UBS's corporate statements and corresponding values of truth, clarity and performance, a financial scandal involving "rogue trader" Kweku Adoboli cost the bank $2.3 billion in unauthorized deals.

# No wonder legal considerations often carry the day!

The heavy reliance on legal advice regarding employment practices makes sense, particularly from the viewpoint of legal practitioners whose core focus is protecting their clients from legal exposure arising out of their treatment of employees. In fact, this view has historic logic linking back to the passage of the Civil Rights Act of 1964 to address long-standing workplace discrimination practices tied to race, sex, religion, national origin, and color. Since then, the factors driving a need to be conscious of legal risks have piled on. Here are just a few examples of the regulations covering many aspects of business:

- Many laws have been passed dealing with a wide range of discrimination areas (Equal Pay Act, pregnancy discrimination, FMLA, and so on).

- States have enacted their own laws addressing topics such as sexual orientation, marital discrimination, and other specific topics.

- With the passage of the Civil Rights Act of 1991, Title VII complaints could be heard before juries and punitive and compensatory damages could also be added. Big cases hit both the headlines and the treasuries of major organizations.

- Several key Supreme Court decisions in the late '90s and after shifted the focus of discrimination claims even further. In their own way, while intending to expand coverage of certain claims, these later cases have given organizations a roadmap for building defenses to harassment claims and another path for avoiding punitive damages. A practitioner given a chance to do a thorough investigation can accurately assess litigation risks and determine whether there is enough verbal, documentary, statistical, or direct evidence of discrimination to launch a case that may be able to get in front of a jury. A lot of cases with unfair and perhaps illegal treatment may never see the courtroom because they don't meet this standard. Acts may have been done with unlawful intent, but they just could not be proved. Some matters may just go away or be settled with confidentiality agreements, ensuring that no one ever hears about them.

The idea that some lawful behaviors can have undesired, unwanted, and unacceptable outcomes affecting workplace performance and results is obvious to most people. But the management of legal risks has, for many reasons, often marginalized what seems to be common sense relating to "legal behaviors." A sort of quick triage has evolved: *If it's illegal, that's dangerous. If it's not, then let's deal with it later.* (But "later" never comes.)

This vision is shortsighted—even in terms of limiting liability because of what the law can't make people do. There are no laws against acts that are unfair, divisive, or demotivating. There are no laws that mandate you treat people respectfully. In fact, there is language in cases surrounding Title VII, the anti-discrimination statute,[3] that clearly states it is *not* a civility code. That is, the law was not written to make people nice. That language may have fueled the notion that uncivil behavior is okay (not just "legal" but "acceptable").

---

### Probing the edges of the law

One side effect of using illegality as your only standard to define unacceptable behavior is that people get interested in identifying the boundaries of the law rather than appreciating its goal.

A number of laws, for example, are targeted at making sure companies do not create a hostile workplace. So I'll get questions like, "Surely not every dirty joke is illegal. What's the boundary?"

My response is, "Why on Earth would you want to find out? What is the benefit to the company if you define a boundary between a dirty joke that may border on harassment and one that doesn't?" Just because a joke may be legal, that doesn't mean it's acceptable.

---

3  *Oncale v. Sundowner Offshore Servs., Inc.*, 523 U.S. 75, 80-81 (1998); *accord Vance v. Ball State Univ.*, 133 S. Ct. 2434, 2455 (2013).

The story of Hospital X's surgeons illustrates why paying attention to legality is necessary but not sufficient if you want to have the most productive workplace you can have.

## The Value of a Civil Workplace

As I described in the Part I prologue, a leader's goal in my mind should be to create a workplace where people can do their best individually and collectively. That will happen only if employees are not subject to behaviors that can hinder their performance and if they have a level of psychological safety that means they will speak up if they notice problems or issues.

You cannot achieve these goals if all you do is follow the law. Yes, **legal compliance is mandatory and non-negotiable in terms of business imperatives, but it's not enough**.

A business leader once challenged me with this question: *what is the value of a professional workplace?* In other words, why do civility and respect matter? The simple answer is that if talent, scalability, innovation, engagement, productivity, safety, integrity, and accountability matter to you, then how people treat each other and how leaders behave should also matter.

Legal-but-uncivil behaviors not only exact a toll on their own, they add to the chances your organization will someday face a lawsuit: First, they contribute to creating an environment where bad behaviors can escalate into illegal territory. Second, they can be seen (especially by juries) as part of a toxic whole once you add in any form of illegal behavior, such as racial jokes or sexual harassment.

While a single racial joke may not be illegal, a pattern of racial jokes increases the odds that those jokes will be part of a legal claim that may have merit. Stop the poor behaviors and you *lessen* the potential for situations to escalate into illegality and lower the toxicity level in the environment. That's why organizations should commit to the goals of a civil workplace and address the underlying issues rather than merely focusing on successfully defending potential claims.

There is a clear difference between organizations that focus on limiting liability should claims be filed and organizations that are truly dedicated to addressing and preventing problems before they give rise to legal cases. The latter have a mindset that focuses on creating a more civil workplace. By doing so, leaders help avoid all the costs imposed by uncivil-but-legal behavior as well as create a workplace where illegal behaviors are both less likely to happen and more likely to be caught if they do. They also gain all the benefits from having a workplace where all employees feel comfortable and know by the way they are treated that their energy, ideas, and loyalty are welcome.

---

### The less dramatic, more productive life of a civil organization

Do you know what helps reduce the risk to patients' lives? A physician who starts every surgery by encouraging everyone present to speak up if they notice a problem or have a concern. Know what doesn't make the headlines? An employee who speaks up about a potential safety problem long before it becomes an environmental disaster. Know what doesn't breed cynicism and distrust? Executives who conform to the same behavioral standards as everyone else. Know what isn't divisive or disruptive? Employees who are conscious of showing respect for their co-workers, who speak their mind yet watch their body language and words.

Welcome to the dull but productive life of a civil organization. That's not to say they don't have behavioral issues. We are dealing with human beings, after all. But when an organization has made civil treatment an ingrained habit, it minimizes the negatives that result from uncivil behavior and increases the rewards of a more productive, inclusive workplace.

# Summary: A Broader Perspective

We need to change the overriding emphasis that many organizations place on workplace behavior, which centers on compliance with legal requirements and treats other concerns as peripheral at best. It's harmful to business performance, hinders building respectful and productive cultures, and ultimately breeds a cynicism and narrowness of perspective that may enhance illegality and related damage. Instead, we need to look at conduct through the lens of organizational values like inclusion, respect, integrity, and teamwork, through which leadership responsibilities and team member responsibilities originate. That's the way to get great results and also operate within the spirit, not just the letter, of the law; in fact, this approach, which includes a commitment to lawful operations, may often prevent, detect, and ultimately limit compliance risk. As I've seen, it can also literally be a matter of life and death in many organizations. I wrote this book to make the case about why this is important and to give examples of the key elements needed to accomplish this transformation.

*Brigham and Women's Hospital (BWH) is one of the most prestigious and progressive hospitals in the world. Dr. Jo Shapiro, who is the Director of BWH's Center for Professionalism and Peer Support as well as head of the otolaryngology division, helped me understand the source of some of the volatility I'd witnessed in highly skilled physicians, and the work it takes to create an environment where that kind of behavior is treated as unacceptable. I think of her experience as the positive counterpoint to the "surgeons gone wild"; perhaps "surgeons gone right" would be a good label.*

CASE 1: BRIGHAM AND WOMEN'S HOSPITAL

# Getting It Right in the Medical Field

"When I trained as a surgeon," Dr. Jo Shapiro told me, "I was taught that we physicians were each to take 100% personal responsibility for what happens in the work environment." There's a part of that philosophy that's wonderful, she added, because it emphasizes the dedication that physicians must have towards their patients. But it has sometimes given surgeons the idea that they can personally control every single aspect of what goes on in the OR and beyond.

Through her experiences over the years, Jo began to realize that's simply not true: the real world did not function the way her training taught her to expect. "My own experience, supported by the literature from both the medical and business fields, is that patient outcomes are dependent on the culture," she said. "I realized our work is completely interdependent. And that is a good thing. The way we treat each other and interact with each other has a direct bearing on not only our well-being but also the outcomes of the work we do."

Her growing conviction that better outcomes would come from better interactions coincided with Brigham and Women's Hospital's (BWH) decision just over a decade ago that it needed to change its culture to improve what is often labeled "professionalism" in the medical field. Jo views BWH's leadership's approach as proactive. "It was true that like all places of employment, the hospital had some employment lawsuits," she explained. "But our leadership was also clear that they wanted a way to help all of us at the hospital simply do a better job."

What was exciting to Jo was that BWH did not come at this from the negative viewpoint of "let's get all the offenders." She said, "We viewed it as an opportunity for us to give people the skills they needed to cooperate."

So just over a decade ago, BWH began its professionalism programs and had Jo put together a center for professionalism to provide peer support. "The center is *not* just a place for handling concerns," she explained. "We do the training and are here to offer peer support—to answer questions and offer guidance. People use our center as a resource for coaching."

The first people trained were the organization's leaders. Now all physicians, physician assistants, and nurse practitioners are required to take the professionalism training as well. "Everything is reinforced through leader behavior and modeling," explained Jo. "We also do a lot of team-based training."

The challenges they've encountered will sound familiar to those who followed the "surgeons gone wild" story: "Where we have the most difficult time is when we're dealing with supervising physicians whose supervisees are behaving unprofessionally," said Jo. Naturally, she added, there is a lot of loyalty from the supervisor to the supervisee. The supervisor's attitude is often *I recruited that person. They are not behaving badly to me.* "That kind of loyalty is very human, and it comes from a good place," said Jo, pointing out that it doesn't always serve the hospital, its patients, or its employees in the long run. "So part of our job is to facilitate more accountability," she added.

In fact, her center is most often working with people who have to hold others accountable. "We have to help them understand the toxic effect of *not* holding their supervisees accountable," she added. "There's a tyranny of inaction. Leaders don't realize how disruptive it is to not deal with the disruptor."

In thinking back over the past decade, Jo advises other organizations to take their own professionalism or civility effort seriously. "You can't do this on the margin. You have to devote resources to it so you can address the real issues," she said.

Jo adds that it's often hard to measure the outcomes from a professionalism program. Her center published some for their data showing positive results from its work. She also knows that the BWH professionalism center is having a positive effect because she knows that people would not tolerate continued investment in something that was ineffective. "Basically, if it wasn't working, I'd be getting a lot of pushback," she said.

CHAPTER 2

# The Uncivility Iceberg

*What you don't pay attention to is hurting you
more than what you can easily see*

A lawyer called to ask me for advice about how his client should deal with a senior leader whose offensive behavior and resulting employee complaints posed the risk of an employment lawsuit—either by the leader if he were disciplined, or by co-workers if he was not. After listening to his description of what was going on, I agreed that a lawsuit, maybe several, was certainly a risk. But it struck me that was not the organization's biggest cause for concern.

So I pointed out to the lawyer that lawsuits like the one his organization might face sometimes make the news but are not catastrophic in terms of legal damages unless they involve a highly prominent publicly known leader (which the executive was not), or what I will call repugnant conduct—behavior that is shocking and repulsive, not just rude and abusive (which wasn't the case in this situation). I recognized that my goal was to help the lawyer see that what would be worse than a lawsuit would be the potential harm to his organization's reputation and the fact that patrons might start to stay away if they found out about the behavior and the impact it had, potentially, on customer service.

31

Once I pointed out these other types of harm, the lawyer agreed they were likely. It's just that he had been so focused on the legal costs that he hadn't really considered any other potential consequences.

In the previous chapter, I pointed out that many leaders fall victim to the "myopia of illegality"—if behavior isn't illegal, they don't pay much attention to it or they delay handling it for a later time, which frequently arrives when it is too late to readily correct. The lawyer falls into that category. His initial approach typifies how this myopia works in two ways to prevent leaders from properly evaluating the risks of uncivil behavior:

1) It keeps them from acknowledging the full range of uncivil behaviors that can pose potential harm.

2) It makes them ignore the many different kinds of costs that uncivil behavior can impose.

Because of these failings, leaders consequently underestimate the urgency of eliminating uncivility or undervalue the gains that come from eliminating uncivil behaviors and the benefits that accrue from civil treatment. In this chapter, I want to fill in the picture by talking more about the different types of harm that uncivil behaviors create and the price that organizations pay when they ignore that harm.

## The Iceberg of Uncivil Behaviors

Over the past few decades, my colleagues and I have worked with hundreds of organizations of every shape and size from almost every sector. When we start looking at uncivil behaviors, it's clear there is a continuum ranging from daily behaviors that are rude and unprofessional to the most extreme behaviors that also raise the likelihood of legal risk. We've come to divide them into four categories:

- **Rude/unprofessional**—conduct that demonstrates a lack of respect or violates organizational standards of conduct, or excludes people from normal workplace social and work-related engagement.

- **Unjust/unwelcoming**—conduct that is unfair or inconsistent, or that makes people reluctant to speak up about ideas, suggestions, or concerns.

- **Abusive/bullying**—any behavior that demeans or insults another person, or that makes them feel threatened.

- **Illegal**—behavior that violates federal, state, or local laws and or regulations.

In our experience, the sequence listed above reflects our rough approximation of the frequency with which these behaviors occur, as shown in the triangle in Figure 2.

**Figure 2: Uncivil Behaviors**

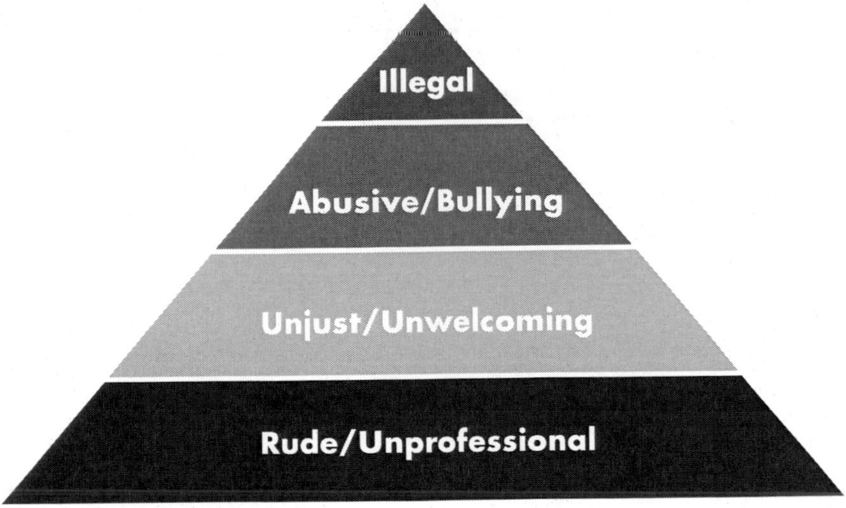

To frame the problem of focusing only on illegal behaviors—the least frequent, top-of-the-triangle category—start first by thinking about the other layers. In fact, pick any of other levels in the triangle and think about what impact those behaviors have on your organization. No matter what level you choose, the consequences are often the same: disaffected employees, low morale, distraction, loss of productivity, reluctance to speak up and contribute, and on and on. Illegal behaviors will have all of those effects *plus* the addition of legal fees and settlements (see Figure 3).

### Figure 3: Impacts of Uncivil Behavior

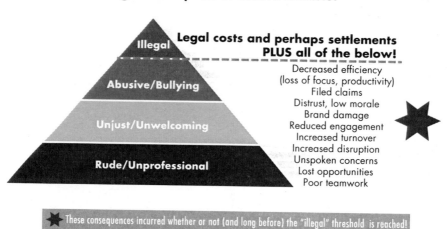

What's important to note is that there is a wide range of consequences—the kind no organization wants to see—*long before and whether or not the illegal threshold is crossed.*

With this new understanding of the impact of uncivil behavior, let's revisit the phenomenon of the "myopia of illegality." This is when the triangle becomes an iceberg: people like the hospital VP in Chapter 1 and the lawyer referenced at the start of this chapter decide not to deal with anything that isn't illegal (see Figure 4). But when framed in the context of the full range of uncivil behaviors, it should be clear that there are significant consequences to "uncivil but legal" behaviors even if we aren't paying attention to them!

### Figure 4: The Triangle Becomes an Iceberg

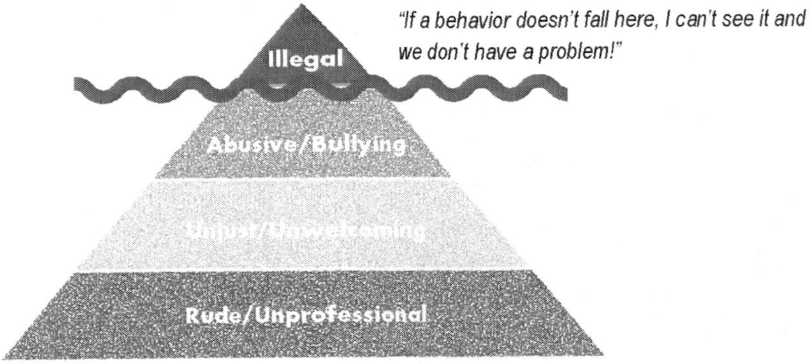

"If a behavior doesn't fall here, I can't see it and we don't have a problem!"

Illegal

Abusive/Bullying

Unjust/Unwelcoming

Rude/Unprofessional

# What Does Uncivility Cost?

Once people become aware of the broad range of uncivil behaviors represented by the iceberg, it's easier to talk about the costs of uncivility and benefits of civil treatment. Executives frequently ask me, for example, how they can quantify the kinds of risks associated with uncivil behaviors. The answer I give them is often eye opening because, just as with the behaviors iceberg, it is the costs they *aren't* paying attention to that are imposing the biggest burdens.

To illustrate why this is true, consider the most straightforward scenario: behavior that is clearly illegal and leads to filed claims and a legal verdict or settlement. Suppose, for example, that you have a manager who flies into rages, makes demeaning comments, and ultimately crosses the threshold in illegal behaviors. The kinds of costs that can occur are illustrated in Figure 5.

## Figure 5: Costs of Illegal Behavior

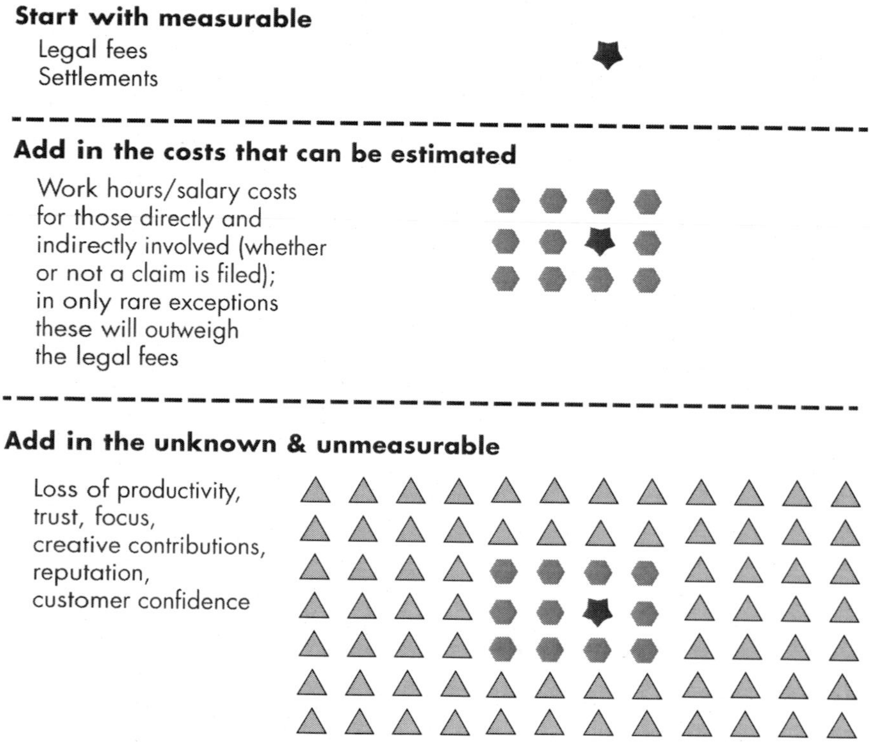

**Start with measurable**
Legal fees
Settlements

- - - - - - - - - - - - - - - - - - - - - - - - - - - - - - - - - - - -

**Add in the costs that can be estimated**

Work hours/salary costs
for those directly and
indirectly involved (whether
or not a claim is filed);
in only rare exceptions
these will outweigh
the legal fees

- - - - - - - - - - - - - - - - - - - - - - - - - - - - - - - - - - - -

**Add in the unknown & unmeasurable**

Loss of productivity,
trust, focus,
creative contributions,
reputation,
customer confidence

There are easily measured costs that such illegal behaviors exact in terms of legal fees, lawsuit verdicts, or settlements (the star in the top portion of the graphic).

There are also costs that businesses can often estimate with reasonable accuracy, such as tallying the time for the people embroiled in the litigation to get an estimate of salary and benefit costs (the hexagonal shapes in the second part of the graphic). They might even be able to get estimates of the collateral time spent by people not directly involved but who pick up the slack for those who are. These costs often exceed legal fees in scope and perhaps even the total dollar amount (except in the largest settlements).

As we just explored, there is a third category of costs associated with any uncivil behavior, whether legal or illegal, such as distractions from work, possible damage to the brand, etc. Some of these costs may be known but unmeasurable (loss of productivity, for example); others you simply will never know for sure and can't possibly measure (such as the loss of trust). And still other costs—such as high turnover—may not accrue from any single situation but can arise when uncivil behaviors are the norm.

Now look again at Figure 5 and imagine that you have the same scenario outlined above—a manager who flies into a rage and can be insulting, perhaps dismissive—but the behavior does not reach the level of illegality or employees choose not to file a claim. The *only* costs that would go away in this scenario are the lone star that represents legal fees and settlements. Everything else would stay.

When it comes to evaluating the costs of uncivil behavior, therefore:

- You can get a quantifiable cost associated with legal fees and settlements, but that does not represent the full costs associated with filed claims.

- The vast majority of costs are incurred whether or not a particular behavior or set of behaviors is illegal (or challenged as illegal).

The situation is even worse when you think about trying to measure the costs from incidents that aren't reported. When looked at retrospectively, it's rare that truly illegal behaviors spring from out of the blue with no hint or danger signals. As an example, consider harassment resulting in sexual or racial misconduct. Long before there is a visible event that could lead to a charge or lawsuit, there might be a signal—perhaps high employee turnover in the form of resignations, or transfers as vacancies emerge. But such a hazard might not show up in internal complaints or external charges in today's workplaces—as jobs remain scarce, employees often choose not to speak up rather than chance overt or subtle retaliation.[4]

Most people don't officially complain about poor behavior from others (especially bosses); they just keep their heads down and grumble to co-workers. These complaints sap the time and energy of the one hearing the complaint and can also "infect" that person. The ill will spreads. And if you've worked in an environment like this, you know that calling it "toxic" is not an overstatement.

So once again I challenge you: does it make sense to pay attention to uncivil behaviors only if they cross the illegal threshold? The answer is obviously no.

## The Costs of an Uncivil Environment

The scenario posited in the previous section focused on the consequences of a single person's behavior. The scope and size of the costs increase geometrically when an organization allows an uncivil environment to flourish, in part because the behaviors that don't cross the illegal threshold will far outnumber those that are illegal. So in terms of sheer numbers, these hard-to-measure costs are much more numerous and almost always cumulatively more costly than the overtly illegal.

Anecdotal evidence that this is true comes from a meeting I had not long ago with a government law enforcement officer charged with investigating civil rights claims. We were talking about his group's caseload and he said that much of what his team investigated turned out to be meritless claims. Naturally, he bemoaned having to spend so much

---

4  EEOC data show that since 1997, the number of charges has remained stable (see http://www.eeoc.gov/eeoc/statistics/enforcement/all.cfm) but the number of retaliation charges has more than doubled (http://www.eeoc.gov/eeoc/statistics/enforcement/retaliation.cfm).

---

## Is there a benefit to uncivil behaviors?

I imagine that I can hear some readers grumbling at this point because I've only described the negative effects of uncivil behavior. Surely, there must be a plus side to the equation; otherwise, people wouldn't engage in the behavior, right?

The answer is not necessarily. When I deal with people who exhibit uncivil behavior, some admit that there is no positive outcome possible.

Others, however, will say that they had the best of intentions: a physician yelled at a nurse because of a perceived danger to a patient, a boss dismissed a subordinate's ideas because there wasn't time or capacity to deal with alternatives. Their point is that their behavior, however bad or uncivil, was a reaction to another person's poor performance used to spur increased productivity or to obtain some other positive result.

While it's true that uncivil behavior gets an immediate result, the nature of that result is debatable and the lasting impact skews strongly into the negative. A subordinate will go along with a decision once corrected, which is what the boss wanted in the short term, but what are the odds that they will ever speak up again, even if they have a great idea?

In short, all uncivil behaviors have a cost and are a detriment to an organization. They have little if any corresponding benefit. So the equation that leaders need to consider when evaluating the impact of uncivil behaviors is populated by many very large negatives and very few, if any, small, short-lived positives. (Furthermore, part of the purpose of this book is to get people to think about alternative behaviors that will get the desired immediate result without incurring the additional harm that could worsen the underlying problem.)

time and resources on so many claims where they could not establish violations—resources that he'd prefer to devote to the stronger claims or use for other purposes.

As I spoke with this official, it hit me. His problem—and, more to the point, that of the organizations he investigated—was as much the meritless cases as it was those that gave rise to strong legal claims. And I thought, *What a huge burden that puts on the organizations he is investigating—they have to defend all these claims that turn out to be meritless!*

Though only the "merit-ful" claims led to lawsuits, all the claims created organizational disruptions and avoidable ill will, and surely affected the concentration and energies of employees who should have been fully focused on their normal job responsibilities.

This official's experience is supported by evidence from the Equal Employment Opportunity Commission. Its data shows that over the past few years less than 5% of charges of discrimination filed have been found to have legal merit.[5] The other 95% were settled, dismissed, or withdrawn—meaning that for many of these claims there was likely some unprofessional or improper conduct involved, just nothing that met a legal definition of damage. (My work and experiences suggest that many if not most of the meritless claims were due to recurring behavioral issues that went unaddressed because the organization did not perceive any legal risk even as they caused organizational harm.)

Ironically, employees who are mistreated to an *illegal* extent are often in a stronger position because the law is on their side and they have a legal remedy (or even the threat of a legal remedy), which can cause the business leaders to pay attention to them and the poor behaviors. Someone who is *merely* treated uncivilly suffers the same frustrations as someone treated illegally, but has no recourse if the organization doesn't pay attention to "legal but uncivil" behaviors—just like the long-suffering staff at Hospital X from Chapter 1.

## Putting a dollar cost on distraction

Many of the executives with whom I work are highly skilled and analytical; they like numbers. They want to be able to quantify the impact of uncivil behaviors as a way to help them evaluate the costs and benefits of investing in civil treatment. So for those people, I pose a

---

5   You can find the data at http://www.eeoc.gov/eeoc/statistics/enforcement/all.cfm.

hypothetical case that illustrates one way to think about the harm of uncivil behaviors that *never* lead to claims or lawsuits (that is, it involves the behaviors only in the lowest three levels of the triangle).

To get a rough estimate of the impact, I'll pose a scenario to executives that goes something like this: An organization that tolerates poor behavior has 10,000 employees. Each year, 1% of the employee population (= 100 people) engage in uncivil behaviors (demeaning and insulting comments, unnecessary arguments, harassment, etc.). The poor behavior of these uncivil employees affects people around them who witness or are the targets of the behavior. For the purpose of this scenario, I'll estimate that five co-workers are affected (100 x 5 = 500 total). The compromised employees lose, let's say, 1 hour of concentration per week. Considering that these affected employees can come from any level of the organization, I'll use an estimate of $50/hr in salary and benefits for the purpose of these calculations. So the math is:

**500 people x (1 hr x 50 wks) x $50/hr = $1.25 million**

If there were any other resource in an organization of this size that was being wasted to the tune of a million dollars a year, I think the top leadership would be interested in finding a fix, don't you?

Though this kind of exercise is useful to help executives appreciate the full, direct financial impact of uncivil behavior, I want to point out that there are other costs to uncivility-driven distraction that are often more important. For example, what if a nurse administering a dose of a potentially lethal medication can't concentrate after being yelled at by a physician? What if a truck driver, frustrated after a bad encounter with a boss or co-worker, fails to notice a pedestrian dart into the street? What if an attorney fails to locate or understand a key case he should have included in a brief because he had been embarrassed by a senior leader in a team meeting?

I understand that organizations want to be able to assign dollar figures to different kinds of risks so leaders can evaluate priorities. But taking this approach with uncivil behaviors misses what are likely the much greater risks. To help illustrate this point, let's look at a few case studies.

## Case Studies on the Impact of Uncivility

To help reinforce the idea that paying attention to the full spectrum of uncivil behaviors, not just those that are illegal, is the best option for businesses, here are a few more examples from my personal experience.

### *Example 1: $2 billion at risk*

I was working with a company that had a brilliant CEO whose grimaces, body language, cutting glances, and sarcastic public insults could shut off a debate in a second or two. One senior executive told me that this CEO's comments, eye rolls, and head shakes convinced him that the CEO did not want to hear *concerns* regarding major initiatives, only *agreement*. Offline, other executives grumbled to me about the CEO and his unwillingness to listen to divergent views, differing opinions, and new ideas.

To find out if this phenomenon was true and how it affected the business, I spoke to a group of junior executives right below the C-suite. I remember one conversation in particular. A junior executive told me he was hesitant to raise new ideas and issues particularly if they conflicted with the CEO's views because he feared the reaction. I asked for an example.

A few weeks earlier, he told me, he'd been part of a team evaluating a $2 billion transaction that involved a major purchase and acquisition risk. Despite having serious concerns that made him uncomfortable about the acquisition, he had not raised any questions during a key meeting with the CEO and senior team.

I asked him why he had not spoken up. He said that he had seen the CEO insult those who disagreed with him and demean their intelligence. The CEO's gestures, tone of voice, and body language were all threatening or demeaning.

We all know intuitively that *words* are a relatively small part of communication. With his *behavior*, the CEO sent a very loud message to his employees: he did not respect messengers who disagreed with him and had no interest in their messages. The junior executive with whom I spoke said that he felt that it would be damaging to his career to oppose the CEO. So he said nothing.

Think about that for a moment. With $2 billion at risk, a person with relevant and potentially critical information had decided not to speak up, allowing a potentially serious risk to affect his organization. And all because of a CEO who felt his ideas were always right and was not interested in listening to, hearing about, or responding to divergent views, and who could communicate potential career danger with a grimace or eye roll.

**Figure 6: $2 Billion at Risk!**

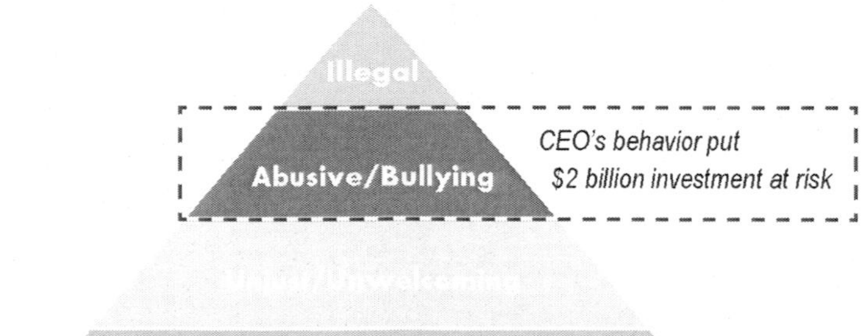

Illegal

Abusive/Bullying

*CEO's behavior put
$2 billion investment at risk*

Unfair/Unwelcoming

Rude/Unprofessional

Various forms of non-verbal behaviors—silent killers, to stretch the medical metaphor—can be toxic at work. The subtle way intent is communicated through behaviors like tone of voice, eye contact, facial expressions, and body language can diminish the productivity of others, affect quality and safety, and thwart other business objectives. And, as in this CEO's case, they can force silence when it's vital for people to speak up and raise the equivalent of code blue alarms. Nothing this CEO did was illegal, but his behavior was clearly jeopardizing $2 billion of his company's assets. I consider that a major flaw in risk management.

---

### Actions vs. words

It's a well-known aphorism that actions speak louder than words, a saying that is never more true than when it comes to leaders. I'll talk more about leadership roles and engagement in a later chapter, but wanted to point out here that the CEO involved in this $2 billion opportunity had written extensively about his company's commitment to values, which included respect and constantly challenging themselves to be better. He had the right talk but not the right walk.

---

## Example 2: Soldier safety at risk

Managers and executives I meet frequently volunteer examples of uncivil or disrespectful treatment they have seen or been involved with in some way. A friend of mine was checking into a workplace problem involving a small team at a specific facility that provides materials for critical U.S. combat operations. The people could not get along; they were mean-spirited and disrespectful in terms of what they said, how they said it, and how they interacted.

I knew my friend had handled a lot of investigations like this before so I asked him what stood out this time. He told me that this team was involved with assembling bombs—munitions used for live combat. The relationships between team members had gotten so strained that it was affecting their productivity, their efficiency, and (I surmised) maybe even the quality of their work.

**Figure 7: Soldier Safety at Risk**

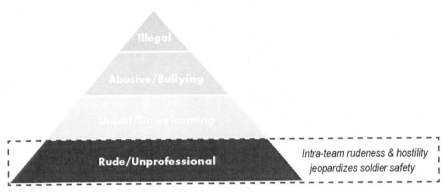

I stopped and thought about how, in this organization, uncivil, disrespectful, and divisive conduct could affect lives in wartime. That was the point my friend was making.

## Example 3: Organizational effectiveness at risk

In both of the stories above, I've chosen dramatic examples to demonstrate just how serious uncivil behavior can be. But far more often the impact is more insidious—just as costly in its own way but less obviously threatening. A small business, for example, had one management team member who was a talented hard-worker. But that person also tried to control just about every decision the business made, and would stifle anyone who tried to participate or who spoke up about issues.

This behavior came nowhere near being abusive, let alone illegal. There were no obvious costs—no $2 billion at risk, no lives in danger. But through negative comments, a refusal to cooperate, and disparagement of others, this executive limited creativity and productivity in the business, and erected silos that impeded cooperation. It affected organizational energy as well—employees went to great lengths to work

45

*around* this executive rather than risk having their ideas shot down without fair consideration.

I believe most leaders would agree that this squelching of ideas and collaboration and smothering of news about potential organizational hazards poses a very real risk to an organization. Wouldn't you?

**Figure 8: Organizational Effectiveness at Risk**

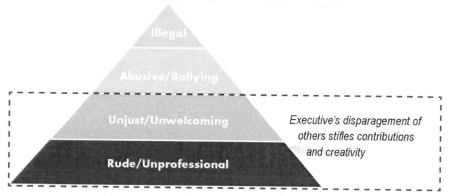

As a postscript for this story, I did an inquiry after the offending executive had left that company and learned that the behavior had spread throughout the team. Some people had spent a substantial amount of time discussing among themselves their frustrations with the executive. A few talented employees came close to leaving the organization's employ.

What I observed in this organization was typical of what I see in many organizations: Leaders whose behavior sets an uncivil tone for an entire organization. Groups where disrespect and divisiveness are allowed to override business need. As a result, many routine daily decisions are affected, not just the large ones. Every day, there is information that is not transmitted or that is simply ignored. Important issues are never raised. People hunker down instead of standing up to share their ideas. And that is not healthy for any organization.

# Summary:
# What *Should* Keep Leaders Awake at Night

What often keeps leaders awake at night are fears about potential disasters. While it's natural that our minds go to these scandals—and all of us want to make sure we are working to prevent them—the odds of something catastrophic happening are relatively slim. The more likely scenario (and the one I think *should* also keep leaders awake at night) is that there are uncivil behaviors going on right now that are robbing your organization of productivity, creativity, and edge, and creating risks around compliance, safety, and general knowledge of potentially dangerous organizational behavior.

The message I try to convey to leaders is that they don't know the full impact of the uncivil behaviors in their workplace, and probably will never know for sure—but it's safe to say it is big! Leaders can count complaints, tally up lawyers' fees, and estimate lost work hours. But no balance sheet will show the full cost to their organization of poor behaviors that go unreported, of great ideas that are left unsaid, of employees who contribute the minimum instead of the maximum. Fortunately, those are costs you don't have to pay if you work to enforce civil treatment.

## CASE 2: FIRST CITIZENS BANK

# More Than Compliance

"When I first came on board at First Citizens, my job was a new role," Lee Hardeman told me. "The company was going through some compliance reviews with the Department of Labor, and there was an existing course on compliance we used, but it had some things that weren't suitable for this organization."

She brought a new perspective that found broad support among FCB's leadership: "As a financial institution, we are very regulated everywhere," said Lee. "But our focus is not just about compliance, not just about legal versus not-legal. It's about what is the right thing to do and what makes sense from a business perspective. A big part of my job is making sure that all of us want to come to work, that we feel good about our environment, and will speak up if we see something wrong. I tell people that it shouldn't require regulations to do that."

As a consequence, Lee was looking for an approach that wasn't just about diversity or compliance. "The whole concept of what you call civil treatment is about the expectations of how we treat not only our associates but our customers and vendors, and how we interact day to day. I don't want our managers and others to be distracted by a culture where people are complaining all the time."

So she championed the deployment of a broad-based civility initiative for the whole company. From the start, Lee knew that FCB had to build a process and system, not just provide training. "You write up a policy, then realize that people don't read it. People say they didn't know there was a place they could go to complain, didn't know what resources were available. In our approach, we needed to have resources in place and communicate that to all employees."

The first phase was figuring out what those pieces were that needed to be in place. For example, she said, "Since we were teaching a class that tells people to get help if they don't know how to handle a situation, we had to figure out how to address that." Before the broader launch, FCB did a day of training with internal HR people so they were prepared to handle questions that might come their way. Reinforcing the training was addressed from the beginning. "We integrated the ideas of civil treatment with other disciplines and training, and provided coaching as needed," Lee explained.

After a kickoff event, leadership training was done first. "We did it as a classroom experience, even though the organization was trying to reduce expenses at the time, and pulling people out of the field for the class can be a challenge," said Lee. "But facilitators and managers wanted the leaders to be together in a room, and that proved very effective." Learning about the consequences of uncivil behavior was eye opening for many of the leaders, making them much more aware of what they needed to pay attention to in the workplace.

Training leaders first was critical to the effectiveness of the rollout. "That made it much easier overall," said Lee. For one thing, when it came time for broader training, "there was *never* a discussion that somebody didn't need this," said Lee. "Since all our leaders were trained, it was clear that this is the way we want to do business at First Citizens."

She does admit there was a little anxiety among mid-management as the rollout reached their level. "We told all the managers that we were going to have a course for all employees, so they needed to know it as well," she said.

What's interesting, she added, was that the managers' first reaction was that the examples of uncivil behavior were "so blatant, it would never happen here." But the training included lots of internal FCB examples. "The managers soon recognized that bad things *will* happen unless they are active in preventing them," said Lee, adding that the same mental shift happened as the training was rolled out to other employees.

It's been several years since the initiative began, and Lee says the working environment at FCB has grown stronger. "Our mantra of guarding our words and actions has become part of the culture. Civil treatment is embedded in how we conduct ourselves every day," she said.

In fact, she added, the company recently finished a merger and they made sure that civil treatment training was one of the first things that happened. "Everyone coming on board, whether through a merger or a new hire, has to take civil treatment training within the first 60 days so they understand that this is our culture."

One of the indicators that civil treatment is having an impact is the *lack* of behavioral issues. Lee has seen this is true at FCB: "If you look at the number of complaints, we have substantially less here than anywhere else I've worked."

CHAPTER 3

# You Can't Conquer
# If You Divide

## *Putting civility at the core of culture*

Imagine that one day your manager uses racially derogatory language while criticizing your performance—which could be one version of the hypothetical situation described on page 35. My guess is you'd be enraged. You'd wonder if you should look up the instructions you once had in a training course on how to report illegal behavior.

Now suppose that instead of the racially charged language, your manager "merely" insults or demeans your contributions in some way, using offensive terms, or calling you an incompetent idiot, for example. Do you think to yourself, "Oh good. That wasn't illegal. I guess it isn't so bad." Not likely!

All of us see and experience behaviors as part of the same package. That's how it is in real life. On a day-to-day basis we don't divide behaviors into legal versus illegal unless we're lawyers, compliance experts, or especially aggrieved. We look at what is acceptable or unacceptable; we can tell whether another person's behavior helps us perform our job or hinders us.

Yet most organizations take a highly complex and fragmented divide-and-conquer approach to behavioral issues. They have an initiative on sexual harassment, one on discrimination, others on scores of compliance topics, perhaps one on values. The list goes on. Typically, these initiatives are developed by experts in a narrow specialty who come up with a long list of important ideas, laden with technical terms that have specific meaning to the experts who work with them daily but not to anyone else. As a consequence, employees get confronted by many standards, directives, policies, and training programs, each of which is trying to teach them a lot of rules, principles, and guidelines using different terms, voices, and perspectives.

The result of all this complexity is "regulatory fatigue"[6] and a splintered approach to dealing with problems that, in terms of how people behave, are connected. People can't remember all the details thrown at them. Leaders are blind to the full costs of poor behaviors because incidents and risks are divided into separate buckets in the budget—or, more likely, don't appear at all on the balance sheet.

In this chapter, I want to get you to think about how to unite all these fragmented issues and efforts under the umbrella of civility and civil treatment.

## Finding the Behavioral Core

As I discussed at length in Chapter 2, the majority of workaday business situations involve behavioral problems that do not result in legal claims. Yet they create great risk to the organization. The key step for avoiding and limiting all risks, legal and organizational, is creating a commitment to reducing all uncivil behaviors and correcting those that do arise before they cause substantial harm or risk (see Figure 9).

---

6  http://blogs.wsj.com/riskandcompliance/2015/05/15/ survey-roundup-compliance-overload/tab/print/

**Figure 9: The Commitment to All Behaviors**

*The task isn't JUST to prevent this ...*

*It is to minimize ALL of this ...*

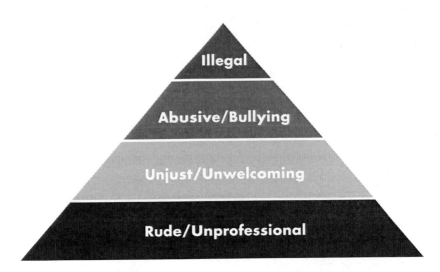

Yet when I ask organizations to describe all the initiatives they have that involve behavioral issues, what I hear is a long list of separate efforts. I imagine drawing a Venn diagram with no overlap between these many topics. I've shown a representative sample of topics that companies mention in Figure 10 (next page), but there are others I could include.

**Figure 10: Divide-and-Conquer View of Behavior**

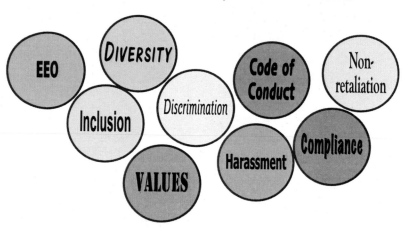

This divide-and-conquer approach may make it easier for lawyers, compliance officers, human resource professionals, and others to divide up and assign communications and learning responsibilities. But the raw knowledge distributed through such initiatives doesn't generally help employees perform better individually or in teams in the workplace. They get overwhelmed and have a hard time making sense of unrelated programs that are dividing topics in ways that aren't experienced in the real world.

When you start to recognize the behavioral link between all of these separate initiatives, you understand it is inefficient and ineffective to look only at illegal behaviors or to treat all of these behavior-related issues as separate entities. All of them are a blend across uncivil and illegal lines.

All of the desired outcomes—a more compliant, ethical, inclusive workplace—are related to core, civil behaviors (see Figure 11). That is, civility or civil treatment is a central, unifying behavioral commitment that must be embedded in many other separate business domains from compliance to diversity to inclusion to ethics to common daily business behavior.

**Figure 11: Civility Core of Diverse Outcomes**

To be clear, I am *not* advocating that organizations abandon their compliance functions or their learning curricula addressing the multiple learning topics required by state, local, or federal regulations. What I am arguing is that all of these traditional initiatives have embedded within them common behavioral principles and objectives about how people should treat one another. They all need to reinforce the key theme of civil treatment as a means of improving business rules, which includes a willingness to raise, listen to, and resolve issues (and, hence, minimize risk, which helps improve performance). And they are all linked to how values are embedded in an organization, which is what I'll discuss next.

# Turning Values into Behaviors

Almost every organization has a statement of values. Years ago, it might have been housed in an annual publication that sat on a bookshelf; now, you're more likely to find it on the organization's website. But having the right language around values is like having the right marketing slogan. It makes everything *sound* right, but doesn't necessarily reflect reality.

For example, Hospital X tolerated the surgeons' behavior despite having the typical values publicized in handbooks, reports, and statements throughout their organization. Yet their values (which included "respect") apparently did not reach consistently into the operating room even though its surgeons' behaviors potentially risked the quality of patient outcomes. Many organizations have run into the same phenomenon: the right words were on paper but actual behavior was very different.

The challenge here is twofold: First, the organization has to be clear about what values it wants to embed in the organization. If your organization already has a list of values, great. If not, use the tip described in the sidebar on page 59 as a quick way to get started.

Second, while the language of values is essentially a commodity—much the same from one organization to the next—the ability to link those values to behaviors is a rarer, more precious skill. So pick a value. Any value. Do you think it's being practiced in your organization? How do you know for sure one way or the other? What *behaviors* are you looking for to indicate whether people are living out that value? By clearly defining behaviors that demonstrate your values, you help employees create a mental picture of what those values mean in everyday life. For example, what does it help to say your organization values honesty if leaders shun or penalize those who tell the truth?

> ## A values "starter kit"
>
> A lot of companies spend fortunes (large or small) trying to figure out their values. My best word of advice is don't spend a fortune of any sort. There is no such thing as a perfect set of values; what really matters is what you do to bring your values to life. In terms of payback, then, putting a lot of energy into identifying values doesn't make sense. Keep that part of your work simple.
>
> Luckily, it's relatively easy to identify values that are consistent with a civil workplace by following the example of well-run companies. Yes, sometimes a company or organization will have its own unique principles tied to a special mission or industry sector. But for the most part companies have the same key values that speak one way or another to the issues of respect, diversity, honesty, and inclusion. With a little research, you can find well-crafted values statements that can serve as a starting point for your own.

## Specific descriptions, specific results

One of the common mistakes that organizations make is assuming that everyone will understand a statement of values because the topics seem obvious or are important to senior leaders. Time and again I have leaders tell me that they have talented staff who know all the technical stuff but were never taught the behavioral skills that could make them more effective. They understand what a values statement says but don't know what it means in terms of their personal behavior.

The truism that applies here is that vague messages lead to vague results. In the same way that telling people to "sell more" is not the same as giving them a quantitative goal, telling people to "act with integrity" is not the same as "don't lie or fabricate records." If you don't provide people with simple, consistent behavioral messages, they will ultimately interpret what you want through their own perspective.

For example, I worked several years ago with a healthcare organization that has an industry-wide reputation for leadership in professionalism. The organization had defined its values, engaged staff, implemented training, and launched an effective communication and education program. But in retrospect, its leaders realized that they had not given specific definition to behavioral markers for items like respect or inclusion; they hadn't defined what those values meant in real-life situations.

They had, for instance, said people should all be treated with respect, but they didn't say that people should not be screamed at (yes, some people find that acceptable) or that if such behavior occurred at a moment of crisis, the person involved should apologize and try to avoid similar occurrences in the future. The lack of these behavioral definitions limited their later ability to hold people accountable when they did not act in a way that would have appeared to fit within the meaning of the definitions. The values violators were able to say: "We did not realize you meant it was wrong to do what we've always done." And they had an argument that weakened the institution's position.

Perhaps it's because of quibbles like these that the concept of defining values and key behaviors—and then implementing them so they have a lasting cultural impact—seems daunting to many organizations. But it need not be, provided there is a clear rationale for each value that ties it to business or professional concerns that impact employees, members of the public, and the viability of the organization itself. That's why it's so critical that values be given thoughtful consideration and that the organization is committed to making them operating standards.

That said, **don't go overboard**. While specificity in defining values and behaviors helps people understand what you want to communicate, be judicious in your details! My company worked with a manufacturing firm whose senior leader has a strong commitment to values. That is admirable, of course. The problem is that in drafting values for the firm, the senior leader selected a wide range of characteristics, about 15 as I recall. He then wrote up aspirational statements—such as "honesty builds trust"—to explain in more detail what they meant behaviorally. This executive's approach posed a quandary for me. Identifying values and linking them to behaviors is exactly what I want leaders to do. So while I applaud the dedication to values, all I could think was, "This is great—except that no one will remember them, which means no one will change their behaviors."

To illustrate the goal of combining specificity with brevity, here's a list of just four values-based behaviors that our work has demonstrated is simple enough to remember but comprehensive enough to cover the majority of civil treatment issues:

- We speak our minds, but guard our words and actions (including non-verbal signals) so that we do not offend those around us.

- We tell the truth and don't lie or fabricate.

- We apologize when we make mistakes and work to correct them.

- We speak up when we have concerns about issues, including violations of our policies and values, and we welcome and encourage other people to do so.

I'm not advocating that your organization use this particular set of statements. Rather, I want to illustrate that it is possible to have a short list that will be easy for employees to remember and that contribute to a wide range of positive behaviors.

Of course, you can and ideally should provide more depth in areas of special concern in your organization—because you want to make sure people understand what behaviors you are encouraging and what behaviors you are discouraging. For instance, take the first bullet above—guarding words and actions. Here are some examples that an organization could give to illustrate specifically what it means by that statement:

**"We speak our minds but guard words and actions."**

- We avoid name-calling.

- We do not tell jokes—in person or in emails/ texts—involving race, religion, gender, national origin, sexual orientation or identity, age, or disability as core examples.

- We respect each individual's physical space—no inappropriate touching or hugging, for example.

- We make sure our body language and means of expression (e.g., tone of voice, eye contact) demonstrate respect and concern for others.

Doing the same kind of exercise around all the core behaviors you want to emphasize will help people translate lofty but often ambiguous values into guidelines that will help them shape their behavior.

That said, there's no such thing as a perfect, antiseptic workplace. So don't worry about being exhaustive in describing value-linked behaviors. Instead, focus on a few key behaviors that will make a difference in your workplace.

# Summary:
# Linking Back to the Behavioral Core

I started this chapter saying that you won't easily conquer behavioral problems if you treat them all separately, divided up into dozens of different initiatives. The way to link behaviors together is through the core values defined for your organization, and the work you will do to turn those values into actions. The implication is that if you are clear about a few core behaviors, you will be able to affect multiple business goals.

To test that theory, I'll play out one of the linkages that is implied by Figure 11, reproduced here:

Let's say that honesty is a core value, and you define civil behaviors linked to honesty—such as the second item in my list of behaviors, *We tell the truth and don't lie or fabricate.* To me, it's clear having a cadre of employees devoted to speaking the truth will either contribute directly to your ability to fulfill the many other goals embodied in the figure or, minimally, help you identify potential problems in those areas so you can resolve them quickly.

Focusing on core values and their translation into civil behaviors, therefore, is how you can unite diverse efforts. In the next chapter, I'll focus on two of the behavioral components that differentiate organizations that are committed to sustaining these links through civil treatment.

*Jason is a Vice President at a major utility.* He and his colleagues have done a fabulous job of making sure that the principles of civil treatment are embedded in the culture—a living, breathing part of how business is done in the company.*

# Maintaining Civility as a Cultural Norm

In some ways, Jason has had an easier time than other leaders trying to imbue civil treatment into a workplace because he had a solid foundation to work from. When the utility company he works for was established, leadership developed a values statement and to this day take action to make those values a reality. The statement lays out how people should treat customers and each other, and how people should respond and behave if they observe something that concerns them. The values statement has become a mainstay for the whole company.

As a consequence, the challenge for him is more one of maintaining values that were there already rather than trying to change long-standing behaviors. One way the company does this is by celebrating instances when people embody the values. "Those are the stories we communicate internally," said Jason.

For example, part of the values statement encourages people to embrace action as a reaction to a crisis. "So we actively respond to natural disasters, for instance," Jason said. The company uses stories of

---

\* The identify of Jason and this company have been disguised upon request.

experiences that employees have had when dealing with natural disasters to help promote the idea internally that "this is how we live." Jason told me, "It's part of our fiber and reinforced regularly."

He described many other ways in which the values statement is reinforced. "During each quarterly earnings webcast, our CEO recognizes someone who has embodied our values. Typically the CEO will call the person, talk about what they do, and share specific reasons why that person's behavior is consistent with how we want to behave as a company," he said. While the official award is given at the company level, some departments and functions do something similar at their levels.

"We also have an internal employee website that has a feature called Values at Work," Jason said. "So our values are ever present in the lives of our employees." The company leaders, he added, are taught to not just recognize and acknowledge behaviors consistent with the values, but explain why. "For example," he said, "I'll send an email to an employee acknowledging something good they did, then link back to our values statement to explain why it was a good thing."

Because the principles of civil treatment have been there from the beginning, the company has not been widely susceptible to the same kind of legal/illegal dichotomy that has plagued the organizations featured in other chapters in this book. "We know that if we are true to our values, we are protected from a legal perspective," said Jason. "We tell our leaders that if they lead from a value perspective they will not only be legally safe but create a more productive workplace."

This mindset is particularly helpful for new leaders, he continued. "New leaders are always worried about the potential of doing something wrong. They wonder if they could do something illegal and not realize it. The answer is that they don't have to be so worried if they understand our values and act from that place."

To help prevent backsliding, the company makes sure that its mission and values are highlighted in their new-leader training. "It's important on Day 1 that we set the right expectations," Jason said. "New leaders get even more exposure. Within their first three months on the job, they have to attend leadership training where they get courses on how to coach, what civil treatment means for a manager, and an introduction to the policies and procedures related to people management and business acumen."

Another part of the company's culture is to connect the dots. "We encourage employees to speak up if they don't see the connection between a business goal or job task and our values, or if they see something that is inconsistent," said Jason. "And it's our job as leaders to make the connections clear or to make changes so that we *are* behaving consistently with our values."

# CHAPTER 4

# What Will Be Different?

## A civil approach to workplace behavior

I was talking with a colleague who has worked for many years on diversity, inclusion, and other professionalism issues. I asked him, "What would be different if everything you are committed to creating was in place? How would employees and managers treat each other differently?" His response: "That's a good question."

It surprised me that he didn't have an answer, but then I realized it was typical of the discussions I have with leaders across a wide array of organizational settings. People often focus so much on the immediate needs and problems that they don't think about what the future will look like. It's difficult to shape a new future if you don't know how it will be the same or different from today.

As I wrote this chapter, I realized I had faced a similar kind of problem in my personal life that has helped me look at the present/future conundrum that businesses face through a new lens. The backyard of my house is bounded by a small lake. In September of 2009, a week of cloudbursts drenched Atlanta and hit our small neighborhood particularly hard. Water spilled over an isthmus of land separating the neighborhood from the Chattahoochee River. The lake rose higher and higher. After an upstream dam was opened, water flowed quickly onto our street. Three feet of water surged into our home, destroying everything on the first floor.

Naturally, I was eager to restore everything as fast as possible. *Let's put everything back the way it was and move back*, I remember thinking. My wife has a design background and had a better idea—to take the opportunity to think about how our future house could be better than the original house. Her first question to me: "What do we want to keep the same and what do we want to change?"

I'm glad I followed her advice. We spent a lot of time planning and devoting thought to what we wanted to keep and what we wanted to change to better meet our needs. Ultimately, we moved several walls, took out a couple of others, and changed the flow of the first floor. The house today is far more inviting and functional than it was before the flood. My wife's decision to envision a better future improved how we live in our house.

As with renovating a home after a disaster, building or rebuilding a workplace culture takes careful thought. What you include, keep, change, and eliminate will affect your organization positively or negatively, likely for a long time into the future. Those choices will determine what kind of "house" your employees will be living in.

In this chapter, I'll briefly dive into what elements typically stay the same when organizations decide to redesign themselves around civil treatment, then focus on critical elements that need to change.

## What to Keep

Much of this book talks about changes that organizations need to make to move in the direction of civil treatment. But I don't want anyone to get the idea that *everything* has to change. In fact, every organization I've worked with is doing a lot of things right, and those elements of behavior have to be preserved. At the top of this list are guidelines around core functions like how to treat customers and following safety procedures.

Next in line are any statements of values that include the aspirational elements needed to create a civil treatment workplace. Some of the statements may need to be tweaked, but generally they cover the right subjects (respect, inclusion, diversity, compliance, etc.).

Similarly, most organizations will have policies that address critical legal responsibilities. In all likelihood, those policies have already been carefully analyzed by legal counsel and compliance professionals, so they should be accurate in terms of addressing required basic ingredients. Again, you may need to adjust the language slightly to emphasize the need to foster more civil behaviors, but the changes will likely be minor.

# What Changes:
# Two Core Behavioral Models

As I've talked about in previous chapters, in a civil treatment workplace, leaders and employees are concerned about *all* uncivil behaviors, not just those that fall within the narrow confines of illegality. The goal is to eliminate behaviors that discourage or hinder people from contributing their fullest and instead create an environment where:

- Employees from a wide array of backgrounds and perspectives are engaged fully so they can be as productive as possible individually and in teams.

- People are able to informally talk about or more directly complain about conduct that interferes with their performance or violates organizational policies, standards, or the law.

- People are comfortable suggesting opportunities for improvement or new ideas.

Achieving these goals may seem overwhelming because doing so relies on multiple behavior choices by every employee, every day. But there are two core behavioral elements needed to successfully operationalize civil treatment:

1) **An environment that welcomes concerns**: An environment where people will speak up about problems and opportunities

2) **Daily civility**: How quickly and effectively people address minor issues (whether potential slights or misunderstandings between peers or raising issues of minor concerns)

While these two behavioral areas are closely related to and build off of the values and commitments that are "keepers," they are often given scant attention relative to their importance in creating a better workplace. Being deliberate about how you handle these two areas, therefore, is what has to change as you move into the future. Here's more about what that looks like.

## Core 1: Welcoming Concerns

I've come to believe that if an organization does not create an environment where all concerns are welcomed, nothing can change in a lasting way. However, where a welcoming environment *is* created, there is nothing that can't be changed for the better, over the long haul. The difference between constructing this element properly is just that critical.

Let me define the characteristics of a welcoming environment with specificity. It's found in workplaces where leaders at all levels encourage people to raise issues that are affected by or may affect job performance or how business is done in their work areas or in the organization in general. It gives the people raising concerns a model for doing so in a way that makes it most likely they will be heard and gives recipients an approach and listening tools or skills for absorbing what they're told and letting the initiator know that they have been heard.

In fact, the best indicator of whether an organization will succeed in creating a civil treatment environment is whether people feel free to speak up about issues small and large, minor and serious, uncivil and illegal. To have that kind of environment, you have to be doing a lot of things right. People have to know that you take matters of civility seriously. They have to know that behavior consistent with your values is acknowledged and rewarded and that behavior that is bad for the organization will not be tolerated. They have to trust that their managers will listen and that action will be taken (even if the outcome is not what they wanted). They have to trust that if they raise a concern they will not be retaliated against, ostracized, or singled out in any way.

While there are many aspects to an organization where civil treatment is taking root, the reality is that if you don't have an environment that truly welcomes concerns of all sorts, you can never claim to have a fully civil organization; and vice versa, without a focus on civil treatment, you will never have an environment that welcomes concerns. There are two key points to keep in mind:

a) **Speaking up is hard to do**: You can't expect people to speak up just because you say you "welcome concerns."

b) **Look to your leaders**: Leaders' attitudes, as expressed through their language and behaviors, will be critical.

## Speaking up is hard to do

History is rife with incidents on scales both large and small where regular people kept silent and took no action in the face of bad behavior, even when it was cruel, sadistic, and criminal conduct. Most of us have the same reaction when we hear that—usually something along the lines of, *That could not be me. I know I'd have behaved differently.*

Yet on reflection and after further reading, I've come to believe that, more often than not, silence and inaction are the norm. It's clear there are too many instances when people have known of hazards and kept quiet for any of us to comfortably believe we'd "do the right thing."

The idea that people won't speak up or act is reinforced by the headlines about poor decisions that led to catastrophes: an environmental disaster ... the loss of life ... public relations fiascoes ... highly publicized product failures ... having a high-profile figure caught in salacious or illegal behavior.

After these incidents, inevitably a senior executive or outsider is appointed to be the "problem solver in chief" who finds that the company had a well-written policy covering the right issues and a well-advertised complaint system. The company can document that the violators received the policies and completed mandatory training. But somebody (or -bodies) failed to act in line with all of the safeguards. Staff say that the systems and processes, training, and hotlines were a joke. People had known for months about the behaviors that caused the harm. There were warning signs—in the form of uncivil behaviors—that showed up long before the illegal or immoral incident occurred.

But one of two things happened: (1) Nobody spoke up; concerns went unstated or were ignored, and the behavior was tolerated even though its severity had long ago crossed from the troublesome and annoying into the realm of a disaster waiting to happen (which it finally did). Or (2) someone had spoken up but got one of the following reactions:

- Being ignored. No one investigated their concerns.

- Having their issues receive only minimal attention.

- Receiving the message, either through direct comments or subsequent treatment, that they'd be removed from the project if they kept complaining.

- Encountering retaliation—being removed from a project or experiencing negative job actions following their complaints.

The advice that comes from a postmortem is eerily similar from one crisis to the next: processes can fail and guidelines get ignored. Getting people to come forward is not simply a matter of systems, policies, obligatory notices, and check-the-box training modules. Even when all the right safeguards are in place, the bedeviling social, cultural, and psychological barriers remain, causing many people not to speak up about or address improper behavior. The human fix is what's vital. And the most important part of the human fix starts with you and your leaders.

## Look to your leaders

Late in 2014, General Motors' lawyers released a report[7] that described how executives and other leaders apparently perfected their own non-verbal communication styles. As candidly confirmed by CEO Mary Barra, GM leaders developed a cultural practice of tacitly agreeing not to pursue business problems with a "nod" while disavowing responsibility with an arms folded "salute." In the case of the Cobalt disaster (a car model linked to numerous deaths), this workplace messaging may have helped deflect responsibility and allowed multiple leaders to avoid taking action to address a serious defect, presumably before injuries and deaths resulted.

---

7   http://www.detroitnews.com/article/20140605/
SPECIAL01/140605001

My guess is that GM's silent communication system started with a few senior leaders, then became so pervasive that people understood the gestures as clearly as if they had heard them out loud. They began adopting their leaders' non-verbal language themselves.

How likely is it that GM employees would speak up about problems to leaders sending signals to keep them quiet? Every organization needs to be aware of the ways in which non-verbal signals are used, particularly among leaders.

Most of us have dealt with leaders whose behaviors are at direct odds with their verbal statements. A leader spouts the company line: "We welcome concerns." An employee with a concern screws up their courage and comes into the leader's office and says, "I'm concerned about something and thought you should know." The leader grimaces or does an eye roll. As the employee starts to describe the situation, the leader is answering emails or texts. Sorting through files. Checking the time. Or giving any number of other behavioral signals that they are

---

### Can GM defeat the silent behaviors?

The unusually blunt report on GM identifies a number of organizational flaws that need to be addressed to prevent future Cobalt-type disasters. Among other recommendations, it emphasizes leadership actions and communications, clearly stated policies, redesigned safety systems, and training. No doubt the company's intentions are serious. Fifteen executives have already been discharged, lawsuits and a Congressional inquiry were inevitable, a maximum $35 million federal fine has been levied, and GM's brand and reputation have been seriously damaged.

Will GM succeed? It's relatively easy to teach people the words to use or not to use, which GM also attempted to do in a presentation designed to purge legally damaging remarks from emails, recorded conversations, and other documents. However, sending long-standing, non-verbal expressions by top executives to the junk heap won't be easy. Getting leaders to make even the more obvious behavioral changes and act on the commitment to civility is hard enough.

not fully paying attention to what the employee is saying. Maybe the company welcomes concerns, but this leader obviously doesn't!

Non-verbal signals are only one way in which leaders can sabotage efforts to create an environment of civil treatment. Employees will not report problems if they don't trust a manager to address their concerns, or if they think there will be retaliation from management if they do speak up.

## How a leader can welcome concerns

The only way you will know if your civil treatment efforts are taking root—and therefore that you are operating an organization that is more legal, inclusive, professional, and productive—is if people are comfortable approaching their leaders. To help ensure that leaders are working to encourage people to speak up, you first have to address the pervasive attitude among managers that complaints are distractions and nuisances. Why do managers think this way? Because *their* bosses haven't made "welcoming concerns" a valued and necessary performance skill. When your top leaders start treating complaints as opportunities for learning and improvement, as a core management responsibility valued by the organization, then everyone else will, too.

As an example of the right way for leaders to welcome concerns, you need look no further than a widely reported story about Alan Mulally, former CEO of Ford Motor Company. Prior to his arrival, people inside Ford had learned not to admit when something was wrong. That pattern continued when Mulally instituted weekly executive review meetings; people were too afraid of speaking up. But then one Thursday an executive had to admit that there was going to be a delay in the launch of Ford's new Edge crossover SUV. There was apparently an awkward silence then Mulally stood up and clapped loudly. He said, "Thank you for the transparency, Mark … is there any help you need from any member of the team?"[8] It was a seemingly small gesture but it signaled a major shift in the company's culture.

Sometimes the behaviors needed to support a culture that welcome concerns differ greatly from the behaviors that managers and supervisors are used to. So it helps to have a model that you teach to all leaders that illustrates how you want them to behave when someone comes forward. Here's a model for leaders that my company developed and that we have helped implement in many organizations:

1) Regularly and informally communicate you want to know about problems.

2) Devote your time to listening to employees.

3) If someone approaches you, agree to talk with them immediately if you can; if not, set a time as soon as possible.

4) During the meeting, eliminate and prevent distractions so you can focus 100% on the employee. This includes turning off cell phones and any other devices that could be a distraction, closing the office door, forwarding calls to the office phone.

5) Engage in active listening—reframing or restating issues to make sure you understand what the employee has said.

6) Watch your non-verbal behaviors, including tone of voice and body language. You want to be careful not to inadvertently communicate frustration, boredom, or disbelief (which is a sure way to shut down any further attempts by employees to speak up).

7) Let the person know you appreciate hearing about the problem. Make it clear that you will do an (informal) investigation and determine an outcome that may or may not be to the employee's liking. (That is, the act of speaking up guarantees that action

---

8  http://www.ftpress.com/articles/article.aspx?p=2065042

will be taken, not that the outcome will be what the employee wants.)

8) Investigate on your own and decide on a course of action.

9) Keep the investigation confidential, but share the resolution with the person who brought the concern forward and others affected by the situation. This follow-up is critical in demonstrating that you are serious in your commitment—that you truly welcome hearing about concerns because you want to take action to address them.

---

### Finding the delicate balance between privacy and trust

In order for employees to trust that it's worth their while to raise concerns, they have to know the outcome of any investigation by their manager or supervisor. But too often in the past, the emphasis has been on protecting the privacy of the offender.

Suppose, for example, that a manager discovered that an employee *was* basically behaving like a bully. The employee is disciplined and is eventually asked to leave because they refuse to change. In the past, lawyers would argue that the outcome of the incident couldn't be made public internally because the person might bring a lawsuit about harming their reputation.

In my mind, however, there is a need to make it clear to the employee's co-workers—and especially those who raised the complaint—that the company took action. The complaint was investigated and action was taken because the company will not tolerate the poor behavior. Without knowledge of what the outcome was, how will other employees come to trust the system?

I'm not saying that you have to advertise the situation throughout the whole company (and never on social media), but those involved deserve to know what happened.

---

# Core 2: Daily Civility Among Employees

When I talk to people about the need to have an environment that welcomes concerns, they almost always think I mean that employees should feel free to talk to management. But the truth is that most daily interactions happen peer to peer: manager to manager, employee to employee. And it is in those daily interactions where the ability to talk about concerns—including grey areas of uncertainty—helps build an atmosphere of trust between employees and prevents minor or perceived slights from growing into ongoing disruptions.

For example, as I was leaving a social event with a group of close friends, a colleague and friend I have known more than 10 years made a painful ethnic comment to me. I knew he meant nothing by it, but maybe my face revealed my surprise. I didn't act then, and wondered afterwards if I should say something and let my friend know that what he had said bothered me. But I hesitated: "If I say something, that will taint our friendship, and maybe that's an overreaction on my part. And after all, it was just one brief comment."

A few weeks later my friend and I were both part of a group lunch. By chance, I got there early. So did my friend. We said hello. Before I could think of what to say, he said, "I'm glad we're here first and it's just the two of us. I want to talk to you. I said something when we were last together and it bothered me. I thought it might've hurt you." He referred to his comment. "Did I insult you? If I did, I'm so sorry."

I could pretend it didn't bother me or I could look him in the eye, and explain why it did. I'm glad I chose the second option. I said, "Yes, what you said did surprise me and it was painful." And I explained why his remark jolted me. He said he hadn't meant it to have that impact. It hurt him that it did. I believed him. I thanked him for asking me. My respect for him as a friend increased. We shook hands and I said, "Thank you for raising this. Let's move on." We have.

We all have our own personal characteristics and sensitivities. We live in a complex society where we have many individual and group qualities, personal issues, identities, and backgrounds. So part of the picture of "daily civility" has to be the ability for employees to speak to each other about things that bother them so unspoken concerns don't poison relationships. And when we think we've said something we shouldn't have, as my good friend did, we need to acknowledge it and say we may have misspoken.

## The how-to of daily civility

In an organization that embraces civil treatment, people have the ability to discuss differences, work them out, and move on. That's what I've been teaching, and I saw it in action, recognizing how difficult it is to apply in practice. When we do work things out like this, our understanding and respect for our friends and colleagues will only grow, as will enduring bonds of trust.

To help build a foundation where people feel free to speak up if they are offended by comments:

- Recognize that communications problems will occur among people of different backgrounds, often unintentionally.

- Teach people how to listen; to give co-workers a fair chance to explain their intentions and allow them an opportunity to apologize, if needed.

- Create the expectation that people will apologize if they make offensive comments, or if an innocent comment or action was wrongly understood or interpreted.

Because these kinds of conversations are difficult and awkward, my company advocates that organizations teach the following discussion approach for dealing with personal slights to all employees. First here are tips for people who want to speak up:

1. Communicate the "why"—explain why you are bringing the concern to the other person.

   > *The reason that I want to talk with you is that I really value our relationship and the work we do together on the team.*

2. Acknowledge the positive intent.

   > *I know we are relaxed with each other and that you feel at ease with me. I'm glad that we can have fun together.*

3. Provide specific examples.

   > *There have been times, though, where you have made a comment that made me uncomfortable. For instance, when _____.*

4. Explain your point of view without judgment.

   > *I realize you meant no harm when you said that, and that you probably even meant it to be a compliment. But it was embarrassing to me because _____ and it made me wonder if _____.*

5. Listen to the other person's response. Give him or her the same attention that you expect from them. (A lot of these conversations break down when the person speaking up has no interest in hearing what the other person has to say! But this is supposed to be a two-way discussion.)

6. Ask for agreement to a specific change you'd like to see.

   > *In the future, would you be willing to _____.*

7. Thank the person for caring and listening.

   > *I appreciate your listening to my perspective on this. I am glad that we are able to work together.*

8. Invite them to ask you for what they want as well, either now or in the future.

> *I hope you will feel comfortable coming to me in the same way if there is anything I can do to enhance our ability to work effectively together.*

Then, for people who are approached, we suggest the following:

- You are obligated by civility to listen and try to understand the other person's point of view. You do not necessarily have to agree with what the other person is saying.

- When you listen, you might hear something that makes you believe that the other person misinterpreted or even misheard your remarks. Explain, respectfully, what you said or meant to say (being careful about your tone of voice and content). Then move on.

If the person who speaks up and the recipient can't find common ground for moving forward, then they should take the issue to the leader, who should be open to welcoming the concerns and helping to negotiate a path forward.

The basic message to send to all employees is that they should discuss issues with others so they can clear up any misunderstandings *and move on.* The sooner an issue is raised and discussed, the less historical baggage it will likely carry and the easier other issues will be to deal with.

## The biggest hurdle: Unconscious bias

Part of the challenge with daily civility is that we're not always aware of our behavior and why we act the way we do. Humans make quick decisions. We're hardwired to react reflexively to strange, threatening, and potentially life-threatening situations. Less dramatically but more frequently, we have routine interactions and later realize we'd gotten a good or bad impression about that person without knowing why. These gut-level reactions often don't rise to the level of consciousness but can affect whether and how we choose to interact with people afterwards.

Articles have been written and tests developed to explain and prove the process referred to as **hidden, unconscious,** or **implicit bias.** Neurobiologists are still trying to understand how it works. What we do know is that unconscious and implicit bias exists and affects behavior.[9]

Worst-case scenario, these biases can lead to bad and potentially illegal business decisions. For example, people may review resumes and screen out qualified people whose background facts may suggest they are African American in favor of applicants with equal qualifications whose biographies suggest they are Caucasian. These forms of bias may extend to gender, national origin, and other characteristics. This process can affect other employment decisions, as well as social interactions.

Even without getting that extreme, unconscious biases can conflict with organizational commitments to maximize the best talents of applicants and employees and to avoid making decisions that are unfair, unwise, divisive, and potentially illegal. To overpower this hardy, hidden instinct, employers have to address it. The ultimate responsibility is to make sure that conscious decisions aren't tainted by unconscious biases.

The power of hidden bias tends to diminish the more we come in contact with people who represent groups where our biases may surface. This is promising; it suggests we should combat hidden bias, especially for situations where relationships are not well formed, and where decisions may be based on qualifications or records without knowledge or familiarity of particular people.

---

9   Nicholas Kristof often writes about unconscious bias for *The New York Times.* See, for example, "Our Biased Brains" from May 7, 2015.

Overcoming implicit bias and improving daily civility is not a simple task; it takes awareness, time, and narrow, workable objectives. After all, we are not going to change the hardwiring of our species quickly! The best I can offer here are a few ground rules:

- Not all implicit biases can be addressed. Organizations need to choose the areas that affect the greatest numbers of the workforce population and can cause the greatest organizational harm. A logical place to start would involve implicit biases tied to race, gender, religion, age, national origin, disability, and sexual orientation.

- Awareness learning should be seen as part of a process, not a solution. You're dealing with deeply rooted processes (hence the label "unconscious"), which is why you need mechanisms that allow people to raise these issues with each other. People need tools and actual behavioral suggestions for dealing with situations where implicit biases are likely to occur. (The model starting on page 81 serves that purpose.)

# Summary:
# The Foundation for Civil Treatment

One of the most serious legal challenges any organization can face is how to respond to employee complaints without violating scores of laws prohibiting retaliation. In an environment where concerns are invited, the response to a complaint will not be the visceral and negative reaction—"let's shoot the messenger"—that spawns many complaints. It will be more along the lines of "let's encourage and thank the person for coming forward." In essence, in a welcoming environment, there's a climate where retaliation is actually taboo rather than an unspoken but accepted norm.

Further, when a welcoming environment is in place, many issues that are often minimized or ignored—meaning the legal-but-uncivil forms of conduct whose impact I explored in Chapters 1 and 2—will be brought to the fore where they can be dealt with and eventually minimized.

Also, when the concerns you are welcoming include minor issues associated with daily interactions, then you have a formula for sustained civil treatment. People will speak up about issues major and minor because they know that their supervisor, manager, or peer will listen to them, that action will be taken, and that speaking up will be rewarded. In other words, listening, action, and support replace dismissal, rejection, inaction, or even retaliation. "Concerns" become a matter for curiosity and investigation rather than fear.

That's why, of all the elements that go into creating a workplace that is more inclusive, diverse, productive, and legal, building an environment that truly welcomes concerns of all shapes and sizes is the most critical. In doing so, you will *prevent* crises and the everyday drag of uncivility, and you'll be able to take action *before* a crisis erupts and suddenly everyone is saying they knew all along something like that would happen!

# CHAPTER 5

# Resisting the Siren Call of the Quick Fix

Once companies recognize that they have behavioral issues that are posing very real business risks—and/or acknowledge the benefits of building a culture based on civil treatment—they start looking around for quick solutions. They want check-the-box online packages, corporate memos, an inspirational speech that they can use to address issues of harassment or compliance or discrimination or civility, values, or whatever else happens to be on their radar screen. Here is a cautionary tale about going down that route:

I was visiting with a friend one day in late 2012 just as two scandals broke. We watched the headlines: The CEO of a defense contractor resigned his position as a result of having a "close personal relationship" with a subordinate. Then General David Petraeus resigned as Director of the CIA after admitting to an extramarital affair with his biographer. Both careers have suffered ruinous, painful, and humiliating setbacks. Their untimely and unexpected departures caused turmoil in organizations vital to our national security.

My friend is an engineer working in the defense community. When he heard about General Petraeus, he shook his head then looked at me and said, "You know what that means, don't you?" I wasn't sure I did. "More training for a lot of people—that's what they'll say," he said. He expected to hear an announcement very shortly, from someone very high up the organizational food chain, stating that everyone would have to go through another online compliance course, review the code of conduct, and sign off.

I had to agree with my friend's assessment. Often in the face of scandal or illegal behavior, the kneejerk reaction is to provide more training. But does anyone honestly think that "more training" would have stopped the defense contractor CEO and General Petraeus? How about the many financial executives who have gotten in trouble in recent years? Or would it have changed the climate in the companies that have allowed dangerous products to be released out into the market?

And let's not stop at the famous examples. Think of people you know who have a habit of saying something inappropriate or acting poorly towards others. Perhaps they've already been put through multiple training courses and others have asked them or even told them to stop. Has it changed their behavior?

The answer is no. Yet still the clarion call for "More training for everyone!" is common in the workplace. Companies want to be able to prove they have trained people in the right subjects and have appropriate policies in place that have been communicated to all employees. They spend a lot of money, make all employees participate, but find there are still recurrences of bad habits (and in the most serious cases scandals, lawsuits, and other serious organizational harms).

In my own experience, most organizations have someone high up who will seek a quick fix to behavioral issues. What I want to do in this chapter is arm you with the reasoning to help counteract any recommendations you may hear that a "quick fix will suffice" to create a workplace where civil treatment reigns. I'll talk about the impossible assumptions that have to be true for quick approaches to be effective, and the mentality that must replace those assumptions if you want to create an environment where civil treatment becomes the norm.

# How to Argue Against Quick Fix Approaches

Just as you can't go completely without food (even if you're on a diet), no organization can move completely away from check-the-box steps even as it seeks to minimize harmful behaviors. Broadly distributing memos and policies and requiring employees to participate in specific training modules are often required so that your organization can prove compliance with regulations (an important issue in some lawsuits) and may be necessary in the midst of a workplace or public crisis. However, just as a short-term diet can help you *temporarily* shed a few pounds, those easy steps don't lead to permanent changes. To lose weight permanently you have to make lifestyle changes. Similarly, you can go on a crash "civility diet," but if you are committed to behavior change, you have to realize that such steps are generally cosmetic: they provide the appearance of change, while underneath the older behaviors are still ingrained.

Quick fixes can support messages when used as reinforcement, but they would only work as the first or sole means of education and enduring behavioral change if the following assumptions were true (which they aren't):

1. If people know what to do, they will do it.

2. The problem is with a few individuals.

3. The issues are cut-and-dried.

Let's explore why these assumptions are false when applied to behavioral issues and creating a civility-oriented culture.

## False assumption #1: If people know what to do, they will do it

Most businesses today hand out Codes of Conduct and policies; they conduct enterprise-wide training that focuses on preventing compliance and ethical disasters. Behavioral standards are rolled out and communicated via one-time classes and/or corporate-wide emails.

I have no problem with these steps *per se*, but if these band-aid steps are the *only* actions that a company takes, they will fail. The theory behind these strategies seems to be "teach it and they will change." Here are the assumptions underlying this theory, and a quick explanation of why they are incorrect:

1) **People don't know the basics**—they are ignorant of what is right or wrong. I will agree that most employees will not remember all the minutiae of legal or compliance rules. But that's not what we're talking about here. The basic principles of civility, ethics, and honesty are so straightforward—don't lie, don't cheat, don't use derogatory personal terms towards others—that people understand what they mean. (Some offenders will claim that they didn't understand their company's standards, but common sense makes it difficult to believe such statements. This holds true no matter what the infraction: harassment, lying, cover-ups, discrimination.)

2) **Once they are taught the rules, people will change their behavior.** The opening stories in this chapter shot down this theory. Nobody really thinks that people will behave the way you want them to behave because they have read a memo or taken one class. Knowledge does not automatically translate into action. We need look no further than the areas of diet, exercise, smoking, and money management to see the difference between knowledge and action! Bad habits don't change

easily—they are familiar and comfortable and that's why we do them. Bad workplace behavior is a bad habit and the same principle applies.

Unfortunately for these assumptions, problems associated with the uncivil triangle generally do *not* occur because people are ignorant of what they are supposed to do or they do not know the rules. What, then, keeps them from conforming to the stated norms? One of the biggest barriers is that every workplace has a significant number of people who have **conceptual resistance** to any behavioral changes associated with enforcing new or existing values. Consciously or subconsciously they will do everything within their power to *not* make a change, justified with reasons such as:

- What you're trying to teach doesn't make sense to them (meaning it doesn't agree with what they believe).

- They do not see the harm in their conduct and may even think it makes them more effective.

- Their behavior is patterned after how they were taught, and they believe they have an obligation to pass the same standards along.

- They are comfortable with the way things are.

- They believe "everyone else acts that way."

- They think the rules don't apply to them.

- They don't care about the rules. ("My personal interests are more important to me than the company.")

- They go along to get along. ("My boss made me do it" ... meaning "I didn't stand up for my own values.")

Often, people with these beliefs do not voice their opposition—unless they are challenged to do so. So you won't know that they are resisting the change until after you've witnessed the objectionable behavior continue or perhaps a serious problem has arisen. No matter how well crafted, clear, concise, or even entertaining, no matter how widely distributed, a quick fix cannot address conceptual resistance.

## False assumption #2: The problem is with a few individuals

In previous chapters, I've given a number of examples of people who violated rules and gave ready excuses for doing so. But these people exist in a context, and in that respect, the organization's environment is equally at fault for the poor behavior.

Many of the organizations I've talked about in this book have the right values, which express a commitment to respect, compassion, excellence, and positive group interactions. They have the right policies published, and top leaders say (and most believe) the right things. But repeatedly, the leaders' tolerance of unprofessional and uncivil behavior sends a message to employees that it is okay to act inappropriately. The leaders do not generally act poorly themselves. But in failing to act, they have communicated that civility (and hence uncivility) is a matter of personal style or choice rather than an organizational standard.

So who is at fault in these organizations? The people who behaved poorly, the leaders who tolerated an environment that made it difficult for employees to do their best work, or employees who were unwilling or felt unable to speak up and raise alarms?

When I examine organizations where poor behavior happens regularly, it's rare that I find an individual or individuals solely at fault. Far more often, I see **systemic** problems such as:

- **Bad examples set by leaders**
  - Poor behaviors started or tolerated by powerful, charismatic leaders have been passed down from one set of leaders and one workplace generation to another. They become ritualized norms; just the way things are done and, perversely, models for how to succeed in the organization.

- **Untrained, uncomfortable, or unwilling leaders**
  - Even leaders who model professionalism in their own behavior often do not feel comfortable with, have the skills to, or see the need to intervene when they observe or learn of improper behavior in others. Because they do not fully appreciate the harm that such behavior causes or the impact of their own failure to address it, their professional bonds with peers and colleagues trump their responsibility to address risky, harmful behavior.
  - They do not talk about the importance of civility, praise good behaviors, address substandard elements, or enforce consequences that could resolve problems quickly.

- **Floundering and inconsistency**
  - The organization knows how to evaluate the value to the organization of particular professional or technical skills, but does not or does not know how to evaluate the value or impact of personal skills. As a consequence, each manager or executive is left on their own to determine what is acceptable or not and to decide if, when, and how to take action.

Having people read policies or sending them to packaged training will not fix these kinds of systemic problems. And as long as these problems remain, so will poor behaviors. If your organization engages in these practices, then you're putting your enterprise at great risk, not just of experiencing major embarrassment (especially in the Twitter age), but also of creating an environment where you cannot take full advantage of the talents of your employees.

## False assumption #3: The issues are cut-and-dried

Blatant cases of misbehavior, particularly involving prominent individuals or organizations, make the headlines. After multiple claims of offensive sexual conduct and harassment hit the news regarding San Diego's Mayor Bob Filner, we didn't have to wait for a panel of pundits to tell us that he had to go, despite Mayor Filner's belief that behavioral rehab would save him. When evidence of racially charged emails surfaced in troubled Ferguson, Missouri, in the aftermath of racial turmoil, it did not take a legal scholar to understand why key officials who circulated them would be terminated.

Stories like these involve conduct so severe that the harm is easy to recognize, and it's easy to rally people around a fix. The offenders lose their jobs. If there are lawsuits, settlement discussions accelerate; the bigger the story, the more likely the case will be settled. With such obvious pain, organizational leaders recognize that their business has to stop the bleeding from an open wound.

Think how much more challenging these cases would have been had there been a pattern of subtler but still harmful and demeaning actions that never reached the public eye. There are perfect examples of this in the Hospital X example from Chapter 1. Here are more of the statements made by the people working with the two surgeons in question:

- *Some are really rough—yelling, name calling, berating.*

- *Some use confrontation as a way of dealing with issues. They "bark at" staff, which is not a constructive or collegial approach.*

Let me ask you: do you think it's clear whether the behavior is legal or illegal? I'd say the only obvious call is that the behaviors are inconsistent with Hospital X's stated values, which include respect and professionalism. Perhaps you think that none of the behaviors (taken separately) constitutes an illegal act. But there is a lot of grey area. Can any of us be certain that none rose to the level of illegality if there weren't also some examples of racial or sexual misconduct (however inconsistent the latter may be)? Perhaps any *one* comment wasn't that bad, but a lot of them together and other evidence cumulatively contributed to creating an unwelcoming or even hostile environment.

Now let's take the challenge one step further. Suppose the behaviors of these surgeons were subtler. What if they just shrugged their shoulders or ignored certain team members instead of screaming? What if they rolled their eyes whenever someone made a suggestion instead of yelling or belittling the person? In fact, one of the comments we heard was: *After a nurse raises a complaint about a surgeon, that surgeon won't talk to the nurse for weeks or months.* The effect that these subtle behaviors had on patient care could be just as bad as the impact of the more obvious behaviors.

Just recently, for example, a young friend of mine told me he'd just changed jobs and doesn't care for the new work environment. For whatever combination of reasons—his age, race, background—he is subjected to daily slights on the job. "But there's nothing obvious," he told me, "so I don't feel comfortable speaking up." I asked him what the impact of this environment had been. He told me that he's hunkered down: focused solely on doing his job and nothing else. "I can see that other people in the office are working on issues that I know something about, but I just don't get involved. I leave it to them to figure out what to do on their own."

If any of my young friend's co-workers had overtly harassed him or discriminated against him, the problem would have been brought to the attention of management and been fixed. But because my friend found himself in a grey area, the organization he worked for now ended up with a disaffected worker and was losing out on the benefits of his full talents and potential contributions.

When people run into situations like these that lack the clarity of gross conduct violations, they often second-guess what happened with great introspection. They wonder if the incident occurred because the people involved either had no judgment or no awareness, or were choosing to purposely skate towards (but not over) a line we all know can't be crossed. They will also wonder if there's even a problem at all; if they are possibly overreacting. In some situations, comments that at first seem improper later reveal something else entirely; behavior that appears innocuous, such as a glance or stray comment, suggests a clear violation of a policy when combined with other facts. In other situations, comments that seem improper at first will later prove to have been misunderstood or taken out of context or, rarely, fabricated by the recipient or observer.

What employee is going to raise concerns with a manager because someone shrugged their shoulders or didn't talk to them, even though, over time, such conduct can be as or even more toxic than explosions of bad behavior?

---

### "Welcoming concerns" about grey areas

Chapter 4 talked about the importance of having a culture that welcomes concerns. That mantra applies to all areas—whether ambiguous or clear. As noted, grey areas have to be addressed or they can evolve into major roadblocks to civil treatment. So do not dismiss concerns about minor issues. People have to know that it's perfectly OK if they speak up about something they are unsure about.

While it may be tempting to simply allow people to *avoid* taking action against ambiguous behaviors, that is not a good option. Left unaddressed, grey area issues can chafe and ruin teamwork, stifle untold contributions, and potentially escalate into clear disasters. Therein lies the challenge in teaching people to deal with uncivil behavior: some parts of it *are* cut-and-dried, but a lot of it contains grey areas that are tricky to define and prevent, and require skill to correct.

## Summary: Finding a New Path

Issues surrounding human behavior are fuzzy. Perhaps a quick fix—whether a slick 30-minute video or corporate memo—can help set the stage for dealing with the clear-cut end of the behavioral spectrum, but I don't know any that on their own can address the grey and ambiguous. Do you? When dealing with behavior, most often it takes more than a quick training module to help people understand when to take action and what actions to take.

True, if all your organization needs to do is "build a file"—document that you have provided a particular kind of training or disseminated information—then some types of quick fix may suffice. Send people to a stock training program, transmit a link for a computer course, have them watch a prerecorded and teleprompted speech delivered by a leader they have never met and never will, read a document, and check their names on a form. Problem solved!

But once the mentality switches from *documentation* to *creating change*, it should be obvious that band-aid strategies are insufficient. Quick fix, band-aid steps are incapable of accomplishing the level of change needed to embed civil treatment across an entire organization—which is the only way that civility can become a norm.

To prevent not only blatantly illegal behaviors but also the detrimental legal-but-uncivil behaviors that were the focus of Chapters 1 and 2—and to create a workplace where civility enhances productivity and creativity—you need a different approach. That approach must be built around a commitment in terms of leadership's vision, resources, and a change process capable of altering long-term, entrenched, comfortable cultural practices. Later parts of this book go into more depth about the elements of an effective civil treatment approach, but first, the next chapter looks at an organization that ran into trouble but figured out how to get civil treatment moving in the right direction.

CHAPTER 6

# The Viral Spread
# of Civility

One of the problems I've been highlighting in this book is the way that bad behaviors can spread from one person to another and even be passed between generations. Fortunately, this viral aspect of behavior can be used to positive effect as well. When an organization makes a commitment to civil treatment and takes the kinds of steps I'll talk about in Parts II and III, good things can happen. This chapter provides details on one organization that experienced both the negative and positive sides of behavior.

## Dire Times at XYZ Manufacturing

I've known Marcia, one of my professional contacts, for over a decade. She once worked at a manufacturing company* with a number of widely dispersed facilities in small towns across the U.S. At the time that Marcia came on board at XYZ Manufacturing, the company was getting a lot of calls to its internal complaint hotline saying that the workplace environment had racial and sexual overtones. The company was also facing a number of EEOC cases. So making the business case that something had to be done about behavior was easy.

---

\* The identity of Marcia and this organization have been disguised upon request.

Based on her civil treatment work at prior companies, Marcia knew it was the right approach for XYZ as well. "I liked the idea of taking a very comprehensive approach. The company needed to address a wide range of behavior issues linked to biases based on race and gender, sensitivity training, and even respect and compliance," she said. "Addressing the full range of issues meant that the initiative needed to work for all layers in the organization, frontline blue collar to white collar. Everyone needed to be exposed to a consistent message that our focus was on how we need to get along to produce the best business results and how we demonstrate respect for each other."

Another key point, she said, was that she needed to set the expectation with XYZ's leaders that change wouldn't come overnight. "Behavioral change is never easy and doesn't often happen quickly," Marcia explained. If leaders endorsed the initiative thinking they'd see

---

### Where morality meets results

The focus on civil treatment is a win for companies on many fronts. Naturally, there's a strong moral argument that diversity, inclusion, and fairness are the right things to do.

Further, civil treatment is a crucial ingredient in a company's ability to grow its business. To make money in the marketplace, you have to have a workforce that is diverse enough to help you **see** and **seize** opportunities. That's why businesses need to focus on all the positive things that go with creating the right culture. It allows you to thrive and help grow your business.

Focusing on civil treatment is also a form of risk management. In the case of XYZ, they had a clear business imperative to create a better workplace environment so there would be fewer complaints and less exposure to legal risk. Thus, building a more civil environment helps a company make sure it is reducing the risks around employment issues.

---

significant results in the first quarter, then everyone would be set up for disappointment.

# Managers as "Viral Vectors"

Marcia told me that one key to effective implementation at XYZ was to teach management first, then step back. "We discovered that it worked best to let management get convinced and become comfortable with hearing and using the lingo associated with civil treatment. Then they could teach the workforce," she said. "So once the leadership at a location had adopted the new approach, it was a quick transference to the rest of the workplace. If leaders had to be dragged kicking and screaming to the table, it was much harder to establish anything at a location."

One reason this worked at XYZ was that it was hard to pull management out of their offices and production staff off the line for the training—especially if people did not necessarily buy into the business case at first. "That's why we started with the operational leadership at the locations where they were desperate to try anything because the situation was so bad," she added.

The way it would work, she explained, is that senior leaders from corporate operations would kick off the meeting and get the local leadership to buy in. Then it became *their* idea. "With this viral approach, we launched the effort with local leadership then let it evolve at its own pace as more and more people began to see the benefits," Marcia explained.

Current employees were then trained in civil treatment, which Marcia made sure was focused on convincing them that they had something to gain. "You have to make sure that every employee knows what's in it for them; why it is important that they change at a personal level," she said. "You have to explain how it will make their day better."

The rollout to employees coincided with a change in hiring to find people who better fit the job requirements. "We then immediately ran the new hires through this training and they immediately recognized that if the company was willing to invest two hours for hourly staff and five hours for management on how to treat your neighbor, then it must care about them and what they are doing."

Within the first year of launching the effort, XYZ trained over 80% of its management and 30% of employees, largely using in-house HR personnel who became certified to deliver the program. This approach proved to have a number of benefits, especially in terms of leadership development and talent improvement. "By getting local HR leaders to become certified and then deliver the civil treatment program, their stock rose dramatically; they become more effective leaders, and were regarded as subject matter experts," said Marcia. "We also created a stronger bond across a diversified-matrix HR organization, which improved the HR function across the enterprise."

---

### Balancing Leader and Employee Training

Having a clear business imperative, involving executive and line leaders, letting the effort sell itself—all of these were critical for success at XYZ. Every company is different and may make different choices, so it's hard to draw hard-and-fast rules about the best or only way to implement civil treatment. But one theme emphasized in this book that XYZ exemplifies is that companies are moving away from focusing solely on legal risk mitigation to *enhanced business performance*.

With that argument comes the need for both leader and employee learning. Think of it this way: Most *legal* risk is caused by managerial or leader misconduct or failure to act. When you're focused on legal risks, therefore, the tendency is to focus only on leadership education and behavior. But most interactions affecting daily performance in a company come from the employees. It is those behaviors that stand a good chance of creating and sustaining a toxic environment.

---

# The "After" Picture

As Marcia noted, "What got me in the door with my bosses and XYZ's leadership was talking about improving compliance and reducing sexual harassment complaints. What *kept* me there was the focus on preventing complaints and improving employee engagement and retention."

She said that after the training, calls to the hotline spiked at first. "We took this as a positive sign," said Marcia. "In our training, we taught people that they had a duty to report something that wasn't right. So seeing the initial spike meant that message had really gotten through."

However, she added, once the improvements in the workplace environment began to take hold, there was a drastic reduction in hotline calls. "At one point we were getting 10 to 20 helpline calls a week, and a year later we were only getting 1 or 2. The company also got fewer EEOC complaints and had fewer lawsuits."

---

### Signs of Change

One of the things that happens at companies like XYZ who put a lot of effort into culture change is that new legends start to replace the old legends. Case 3 on the utility company was a classic example: new stories about people exhibiting civil behaviors start to dominate.

As another example, I recently listened to a CEO speak about how critical integrity and customer service were to his company. He gave an example of how his team had resolved a serious issue at great cost to the organization because it was the right thing to do even though his company was not responsible for the error. I got his point and will remember it. Others did and will, too. People remember stories more than facts or phrases.

At my own company we have stories about people who stepped in at short notice to help out in a crunch, demonstrating their commitment to the organization and each other. We have other stories about people who spoke up about problems; about people who treated others well. I tell those stories often, both in informal conversations and formal staff meetings. That kind of practice is how culture is built and maintained.

---

One of the best indicators that the situation at XYZ had changed was that employees began recommending that friends and relatives apply to work at there. "They weren't doing that before. Our plants were places where people expected to come, work really hard, make a lot of money, and then leave. Now, people are telling their friends, 'You have to come here, it's a great place to work.'"

## Summary: How Positive Behaviors Stick

What I like most about the experiences that Marcia described for me is how dramatic the change was in XYZ's culture. As she says, it didn't happen overnight. But within two years the everyday experiences of employees was dramatically different. Women and minorities in particular could come to work and contribute their best, no longer experiencing the near-constant threat of being subjected to harassment. Just as the poor behaviors had spread at some point in the past, civil behaviors had a "stickiness" of their own. They spread virally because leadership was constantly involved, people were widely trained, and issues got raised and discussed rather than swept under a rug.

Another theme I like to point out is that these cultural changes had a variety of business impacts. First, there was the reduction in risks associated with lawsuits. Second, XYZ didn't have to give up it's reputation as *the* place to work in these small town. In fact, it became even more attractive to employees. Only now, the company gets a lot more return on the investment in high wages because employees want to stay; they are no longer in a hurry to make a pile of money and leave. I don't know any company that wouldn't relish the chance to reduce turnover and avoid the costs incurred when trained, experienced employees leave.

# What Kind of Legacy Do *You* Want to Leave?

nother aspect of the Hospital X story (in Chapter 1) that stuck with me for many years is a one-on-one interview I did with the most challenging of the two surgeons. He recognized that he was known as a superb surgeon and admitted to me that he had a range of behaviors that were problematic, including displays of anger, screaming, ignoring others, and rudeness (interrupting people or not listening).

I asked this surgeon to tell me about how he had gotten that way. "I learned from the best," he said. What he meant was that he'd been taught both his surgical techniques *and behavior patterns* from a renowned surgeon who was his mentor.

A few months ago, I tracked down the biography of this mentor surgeon, which took me down a path that gave me more insights into how culture originates and how it is perpetuated through leaders as role models. It turns out the mentor surgeon was part of a traceable lineage of poor-behaving but brilliant medical practitioners. Here's a brief recap of what I learned:

- In the late 1800s and early 1900s, Johns Hopkins was at the forefront of a move to develop new standards of medical care. It recruited four top-rated doctors, one of whom was William Stewart Halsted, who popularized sterile procedures and anesthesia and developed a number of surgical techniques that lasted for decades and are present in some form even today.

- According to a biography of Halsted[10] and other accounts, he was indeed a brilliant doctor, but also remote and difficult to work with, perhaps in part because of an addiction to cocaine and morphine. But people tolerated his poor behavior, presumably because of his contributions (and maybe the times as well).

- One of Halsted's most noteworthy trainees was Harvey Cushing, the father of neurosurgery. Cushing couldn't tolerate Halsted's behavior and left to become the first surgeon-in-chief at Peter Bent Brigham hospital (which eventually became Brigham and Women's Hospital).

- Interestingly, Cushing exhibited some of the behavioral traits that he despised in Halsted. One of Cushing's residents said that working for Cushing was more stressful than being at Gallipoli (possibly the most horrific battle of its time).[11]

Halsted and Cushing were passionately committed to doing what was right for their patients, and along the way made great advances in medical techniques. But at the same time they exhibited behaviors that studies have proven impede communication and can even lead to complications and fatalities, thus posing a risk to patient outcomes.[12] As it turns out, the surgeon I interviewed could trace the professional lineage of his training back to Halsted and Cushing. It struck me that he was likely perpetuating a long line of behaviors that had been deemed acceptable in his profession.

10 Gerald Imber, *Genius On the Edge: The Bizarre Double Life of Dr. William Stewart Halsted,* Kaplan Publishing, 2011. ISBN-13: 978-1607148586

11 Michael Bliss, *Harvey Cushing: A Life in Surgery,* Oxford University Press, 2005. ISBN-13: 978-0195329612

12 Whittemore, Anthony D., M.D. "The impact of professionalism on safe surgical care." Journal of Vascular Surgery 45(2): 415-419. February 2007. http://www.sciencedirect.com/science/article/pii/S0741521406019719

In sum, Halsted's and Cushing's legacies were twofold:

1) They are widely acknowledged for inventing modern practices of surgery that have saved countless lives and improved patient care for more than a century.

2) They also fostered an inheritance of poor, aloof, or dismissive behavior that has been passed down just like DNA from generation to generation.

What I find most interesting is that Halsted's and Cushing's legacy of modern surgical practices has continued to evolve and be improved. But apparently the transmission of poor behavior is far more resistant to improvement!

Part of my mission now is to help leaders avoid creating a Halsted/Cushing behavioral legacy, which may include uncivil behavior by today's standards. It starts by having them acknowledge that toxic behaviors occur in their workplaces and recognize for themselves the way those behaviors prevent their organizations from achieving critical objectives.

I then challenge them to think about *why* they allow uncivil behaviors to continue—especially because **uncivil behaviors confer no benefit to the organization**. They are harmful to plans and visions, harmful to the goals of productivity, inclusion, diversity, and a host of other attributes you want your organization to have. Plus, fixing them will cost relatively less compared with capital outlays that organizations often encounter.

In that spirit, I urge you to think about the business and operational goals you want to achieve, and what your workplace needs to look like—how it needs to function—to support those goals. Making that vision a reality is the subject of the rest of this book.

*Part II*

# Persuasion vs. Communication

# Teaching so People Will Learn and Act

A senior leader told me he wanted to change the behavior of key staff who habitually engaged in unprofessional and perhaps even abusive conduct. (Sound familiar?) "Why don't we put them all through an e-learning module or two?" he said. "By letting them do this on their own schedules, we'll be able to roll this out quickly."

"Because it won't work," I replied. If you've read the preceding chapters, you can probably guess what I explained to him.

Some companies invest a lot of time and effort in education when rolling out a new initiative—many, if not all, employees are required to take time off the job to participate in some form of education or training. This mass inoculation is simple from the standpoint that no one has to think about what is going to be most effective for different audiences and what will have the greatest impact in terms of changing behavior. The primary driver is "how can we get the message out quickly with the least disruption to our employees?"

Organizations that are focused solely on legal issues often don't look at the value they want to achieve, or they assume that the value is in just doing the training and documenting it. It doesn't take an effective educational effort if a company just wants to build legal defenses if there is a claim and be in a position to argue that punitive damages should not be awarded. Documenting compliance training may help prevent some lawsuits, and will help them defend and settle others. In the same way, a lawyer just needs to prove they completed a course to maintain their license. The only requirements in these circumstances are that accurate information on the selected subjects is sent out and attendance is documented. There's no reason to invest a lot as you'll serve your purpose and obtain your value with minimum effort.

The mentality around education and training shifts quite a bit when the goal is improving the working environment so you can prevent not only illegal but uncivil and unprofessional behavior, which shifts the priorities when it comes to communication and education. When you want to change the behavior of people who are generally comfortable doing things the way they have always done them, communicating information is the easy part of the job. The hardest part by far is **persuading people to change**.

Think for a moment about what that means in the context of Hospital X's surgeons-gone-wild experience. The bad behavior of the two surgeons is easy to describe in terms of what they did and how they acted; and proper corrective standards should likewise be easy to identify. But their conduct (and that of others like them) has almost always been prompted by a motivation to provide excellent care to patients. The hospital doesn't want the surgeons to lose that motivation, but needs to help them see how their behavior is preventing others from providing the best care possible, and then help them develop alternative (and more effective) ways of achieving their goals. It needs to provide them (and others like them) a reason to change that is greater than the motivation to keep doing what they are used to doing.

Let's talk about how education and communication can help in this regard. Looking at the benefits you expect from an educational effort as you consider how to educate leaders and employees is key. Understanding the goals will affect the media you used for communication, how message will be reinforced back on the job, and how, over time, the messages will be sustained. Understanding these factors is critical at the outset; you have to pay attention not just to *what* will be taught but *how*. The art of the process is figuring out a strategy so the learning will be absorbed, retained, understood, and embedded not only in people but in the collective consciousness of the organization—that is how education fits into culture change.

Though education alone is not the solution to uncivil behaviors, it does play a central role in any effort to improve civil treatment; unfortunately, organizations are prone to making a number of mistakes around education linked to behavior change. So I wanted to devote some space to the issue of education and its ultimate purpose: applied learning that leads to a civil treatment workplace. In the following chapters, I'll point out a few of the common ways that educational efforts fail, present some "commandments of learning" that help prevent those failures, and talk about how to think through the issue of educational strategies.

# CHAPTER 7

# Make It Matter.
# Make It Simple.
# Make It Stick.

Dealing with education intended to support culture change can seem complicated and even overwhelming at times. There are multiple issues involved; you have to deal with subtleties and grey areas; and, after all, you're trying to change behaviors that are often broadly accepted even among those who don't necessarily behave that way themselves. Here's a mantra we use to lay out what needs to be done so that learning has a lasting impact on how people act at work: **Make it matter. Make it simple. Make it stick.**

In this chapter, I'll walk through each of the three elements—matter, simple, and stick—and provide more context about what it means, why it's important, and how you can achieve it.

## Make It Matter

People are most likely to pay attention to content when it is positioned in a way that matters to them. Part of the learning process must convince them that the lessons are important. With all the data we constantly receive, most of us just don't have time to focus on information that has no significance to us in terms of our jobs or our own personal opportunities and risks. It's easier to discard information than it is to absorb and apply it. Just because content is important to the organization or the instructor doesn't mean that the learner will see it the same way.

Remember, a lot of the behavior that organizations want to change doesn't feel wrong to those who exhibit it. For example, I've heard about socialization rituals at a number of organizations that sound a lot like fraternity hazing gone too far. The intention may be good—existing employees want new employees to feel like part of the family—but the actual ritual can disaffect as many (or more) people as it integrates. The people carrying out these long-held rituals are not going to immediately recognize that what they are doing is inconsistent with civil treatment, so the behavior will persist until they recognize the negative impacts and have a compelling reason to change.

One of the first issues you have to think through, therefore, is how to explain the need for change in a way that resonates with people personally. What you teach people and weave into your business—be it about civility, compliance, harassment, or anything else—must **matter to them**. It must apply to real responsibilities, benefits, and risks, not obscure, abstract contingencies. That typically means you need to tie the changes you are asking of people to one of the following topics:

- Personal safety or personal financial risk

- Teamwork

- The company's performance

- The job

- Personal or criminal liability

- Effectiveness

- Reputation

- Opportunities for advancement

- What your leaders demonstrate an interest in through their behavior

- Impact on customers (by whatever name you call them—clients, patients, etc.), other members of the public, and co-workers

A word of caution here, however: Be careful about just tossing out a litany of topics hoping that your audience(s) will see a link to their behavior. Make sure you find out what really matters to them and link the behavior issues to a risk posed to that core topic.

Making organizational values matter is also related to how you communicate the new ideas. Simply stating the principle won't do it. You need to provide stories and examples that are germane to the audience and talk about the impact of the values and behaviors on the person and the organization. You need to deliver the messages in a way that allows people to discover and understand for themselves why issues are important to them, their work group, and the organization.

## Make It Simple

I once met with the person who was in charge of diversity for a large, global consumer products company. To help staff deal with all of the issues that arise in a global company, he'd developed a 7x7 matrix of competencies—49 different combinations of situations and tactics that he expected people to learn. It was obvious to me that was too complicated. Employees in this company would need a Ph.D. in international relations just to hold a meeting! I'm sure that few employees remembered anything at all about this matrix.

I'll contrast that experience with another I had in London when I saw a sign in an office window (top of next page). I stopped, read it, and got it. I was struck by the clarity and simplicity of the message. Namely,

(1) if you want a job you better get this message, (2) they won't even consider you unless you have boots and a vest, and (3) they mean it and will enforce these standards. People who read the sign could decide if

**No boots
No vest
No job** CODE

they wanted to conform to the rules in order to be considered for a job.

The message is very clear and simply communicated. Those are the same goals I have for communication associated with a civil treatment initiative.

I once met with both a general counsel and an executive vice president at a prestigious retailer. I asked them how they manage ethics and related issues. They said, "It's sort of a back-of-the-envelope kind of thing. Our CEO talks about it, we all talk about it, we send out quizzes, and we do training; we're always communicating." They said more and more people bring them issues that they can help resolve. I told them they have it right. Simplicity and repetition from leaders trump complex information assaults and mazes of rules.

Each of us takes in a lot less information than is transmitted to us. We can only absorb so much, even in the context of highly engaging experiences. Lots of details fall through the cracks in our attention. Retention of learned information falls off dramatically within hours and days of a training event. And over time, retention continues to decline.[13]

Think back to your own educational experiences. Have you taken a class, gone through a webinar, or completed an online module more than a week ago? Quick—don't check your notes or review the syllabus—what do you remember? My guess: the more complex and

---

13 Read *Moon Walking With Einstein: The Art and Science of Remembering Everything* by Joshua Foer to learn more about this. The Penguin Press, 2011. ISBN-13: 978-0143120537

detailed the topic, the less likely it is you recall much of what you were taught. And if you've only used the information once and heard little or nothing about it since, you'll likely remember less. That's how perception, memory, and learning work. Give people too much information, present them with too many topics, lay out too many matrices setting behavioral standards and rules, inundate them with laws, and ultimately it all gets lost. People will think, "This is too much to absorb on top of my job. I've got other things to worry about."

So the *more* expansive the list of behaviors you want to teach people, the *less* likely the key ones will stand out and be remembered. To get through all of this noise we need to do more with less—in terms of how leaders lead, the standards we set, what we must learn, understand and apply, and how we act and communicate. We need to work with less so we can do more to set standards and prevent, detect, and correct problems while remaining faithful to our values and missions.

Our failure as human beings to retain much of what we initially learn is also why reinforcement is a critical element if you want the lessons you teach to take hold in the workplace, as I'll discuss next.

## Make It Stick

From time to time, my conversations with prospective clients go like this: "They're simply not getting it," an executive will tell me. "We give our leaders and employees great training videos to watch. We have them go to classes that address our issues. We deliver engaging e-learning and we send them reminders. But something's not working. Not enough are getting key points and applying what they're supposed to learn. Managers, executives, and employees are saturated with information and they're zoning out. How do we fix this?"

In the last 25 years, I've heard this frustration expressed about educational initiatives on topics ranging from discrimination to abusive conduct, to encouraging the raising of concerns, to ethics and compliance responsibilities. The challenge is keeping the learning alive after an initial event. Behavioral change is a daily process, so you have to find a way to keep the lessons present in daily work lives.

Start by acknowledging that anything that is important enough to teach is important enough to reinforce. Otherwise, it will be quickly forgotten. If the subject is not important enough to make sure it is applied, then address the deficiency like any other issue that involves rote learning: by giving employees ready access to information on details you don't expect them to remember. Because this notion of "stickiness" is so important, and so integrated with the concept of true learning, I'll talk more about reinforcement in the next chapter.

## Summary: Three Simple Words

A main factor contributing to the problem of poor behavior is that we've made ethics, compliance, and daily behavioral standards too complex. By trying to convey too much, we accomplish too little. Thus "teach little, remember much" is a better mantra than "teach much, remember little."

The more effective approach is to be as brazen in our simplicity and consistency as the scandals we are trying to prevent. We need to establish a few limited rules with clear language, explain the consequences to the person and the business of violating these rules, enforce them, and then repeat the pattern over and over again.

Rather than get trapped into a pattern of overwhelming complexity, make my motto your new mantra: Make it Matter. Make it Simple. Make it Stick. Applying that simple phrase to any change and learning initiative will help translate your values and goals into enduring behavioral and cultural change.

CHAPTER 8

# Using Education
# to Foster Culture Change

Nearly every sector of academia, healthcare, other professional fields, and the business world is filled with examples of ineffective instruction—learning that does not achieve the intended goal. Here's one such example: I was meeting with the general counsel for a large firm, and he had a very specific concern related to a compliance issue. He was surprised to realize that many managers in his company did not understand why they must act when made aware of policy or rule violations. "How could our managers not understand?" he said. "For years, we've been requiring them to complete a battery of online training."

It occurred to me that this lawyer was likely an apt student. Learning in a classroom setting came naturally to him, so he assumed that having people attend a class was enough; nothing else had to be done. For most of us, however, passing along new ideas is rarely as simple as providing one classroom session. In fact, that approach never succeeds if the goal is to develop new skills and change long-lasting habits. I pointed out to the counsel that his company's training was crammed with ideas and legal terms, and I guessed that many managers saw completing the training as an unwelcome prerequisite to keep their jobs. "People don't pay attention in those circumstances and even if they hear the words and write them down, they may not understand how to apply them in their daily work lives," I explained to him. "And the more complicated and detailed the lessons, the less people will remember."

Here's another learning fail: I remember sitting in a cavernous auditorium with 14 other Georgia attorneys. The lawyer in front of me was doing a crossword puzzle; the lawyer to his left was scanning her tablet. Several were sending emails; one was reading a crime novel, another, a newspaper. One was sound asleep. The remaining three or four people were watching a panel of distinguished attorneys discuss regulatory issues via a live video feed. The presentation reminded me more of a freshman college lecture than a professional seminar.

Most of us in that room were scrambling to complete our compulsory legal education hours for the year. By the end of the day, each of us had accrued six hours of course credit: half the number we needed to maintain our deeply valued bar licenses.

Thousands of lawyers in Georgia go through this drill every year. It is the norm of training in our profession. It may not be true of every course offered or of every lawyer attending, but the pattern of seeing people sitting in their seats complying but doing nothing else is common. We're like millions of employees who plant their bodies in front of a droning instructor, an online click-through course, or a remote broadcast needed to complete required programs and qualify for bonuses or perhaps even just remain employed. Nothing much meaningful comes from these drills.

These three stories illustrate a fatal flaw in much training: it ignores the difference between **spreading information** (and documenting its receipt) versus **delivering learning with the purpose of creating sustained behavioral change**. Publishing a document of rules is not the same as learning. And even learning—absorbing information—is not the same as applying knowledge by changing behavior.

Some companies still have courses that are as deadly boring as the dullest of college lectures you can recall. Others have invested a lot of time and money to make sure their training courses are entertaining. They may involve games, skits, or comedic routines. But simply passing along facts and data—even in an entertaining mode—doesn't affect behavior. We have many experiences that are interesting, engaging, and perhaps even captivating, but it doesn't lead to sustained changes in behavior, especially when the target is habits with which people are comfortable.

There is much more to creating a civil workplace than training or education. But the whole picture can crumble if you don't have a solid learning program at the core, which is the subject of this chapter. I'll cover the two rules that apply to every learning strategy and provide additional tips that my company has found help to increase the effectiveness of educational programs.

# The 1st Rule: Make It a Process, Not an Event

In the workplace, the expectation is that people will apply new knowledge on the job. To make that happen, you can't rely on a one-time event, be it a live class or online learning. Knowledge gained in a classroom or formal training is not enough to change behavior, so you need to think about learning as a process that engages people in multiple ways over time. It takes repeated exposure to ideas in different modes and contexts, and opportunities to practice and improve skills, for people to start behaving in different ways.

That means you'll need to approach the educational component of civil treatment by thinking of a sequence of activities that will achieve your goals. Start with how the initiative will be communicated and what the initial learning experiences will be like. People should not just passively read information but be allowed to observe *and practice* new skills.

You'll also need to think about multiple forms of reinforcement because people are more likely to absorb and apply the things they see practiced and hear talked about on a *regular basis* than anything they hear in a one-time or annual class. So consider how to deliver additional content that includes refreshers of key themes throughout the course of the year. All of this needs to be planned, managed, and measured, not left to chance.

## The 2nd Rule: Make It Experiential

People are most likely to remember something that is attached to an experience that happens to them or that is personally meaningful. That's why any approaches you use to spread civil treatment have to create experiences and be positioned in a way that matters to people as learners. (And to revisit a point made earlier, by "experiences" I don't mean simply entertaining people. I mean engaging them in simulations where they go through the experience of trying to apply new perspectives and principles to an actual or true-to-life situation.)

The effectiveness of experience-based learning came home to me years ago in my work as legal counsel. Knowing how stressful the cross-examination experience can be, I always warned clients what could happen if they said certain things or exhibited certain behaviors when on the witness stand. To drive the point home, I started doing brief simulations with my clients before we went into court. When they got to practice being questioned by me or other counsel, or to pretend to be part of a jury observing a witness being cross-examined, they understood intuitively how hard it was to answer questions and how likely it was that people sitting right next to them could interpret facts differently. That experience demonstrated the risks of being on a witness stand much more effectively than any lectures I gave them. If they chose to go forward, they at least had a real sense of the legal risks they could face, the importance of acting properly, and also the need for them to get help if they made a mistake.

In the context of training leaders on their legal responsibilities (part of the periodic sessions many lawyers provide to their clients), I started adding simulations and focusing on core behaviors to prevent liability. When I made that change, it became much easier to get the leaders' attention. Such simulations are engaging and, at times, thrilling for the participants—though not necessarily a positive thrill if they're the ones being questioned. They are meaningful because participants are the ones who say, "That's an experience I don't want to have in the real world, and I'm glad I learned it here." They see how their behavior will matter in a world outside the classroom or the workplace. They became convinced, as I've said for many years, that it's far better to learn in a classroom than a courtroom!

The usefulness of simulations has carried forward into the work my colleagues and I now do. We've seen that they are very effective for teaching behavioral issues—including safety, quality, efficiency, communication, reputation, recruitment, and teamwork, among other business necessities. Through simulations, participants get to observe **behaviors in action,** both good and poor. We structure the simulations so participants learn the rationale for change and are taught exactly what they are expected to change. They also get the chance to practice new skills. Learning without practice is information without application; practice without learning is application without relevance.

As you develop your own educational modules, the simulations or other experiences you develop should give your learners a chance to recognize and identify for themselves the consequences—positive and negative—of both civil and uncivil behaviors. That is a far more effective learning strategy than simply lecturing them. The positives and negatives need to be presented in a context that matters to them in their jobs. They must be real and concrete, not an abstraction or remotely theoretical.

---

### Is a formal learning experience needed at all?

Before you launch an educational effort, consider this key question: *is a formal learning experience needed at all?* Do people have to go to a classroom or log into a website to sit through a presentation that someone else has prepared? The answer is not always yes.

If you are simply delivering information in a one-way, passive process, that is not training. It will not build skills or change behavior. Rules, processes, policies, and standards are data—information that can be stored and readily accessed. It's important for people to know the basics and how and where to get access to details when needed, and to be periodically reminded what to do or not do. Getting people to watch videos and click through information screens is basically a communication initiative, not a learning exercise. If all you need to do is communicate information, the process can be handled via a one-way release of memos, PowerPoint slides, short videos, or other similar means.

---

## Tips on Effective Instruction

The two rules just covered—treating learning as a process and making it experience-based—are the most important guidelines I can offer when it comes to creating learning programs that will change behavior. In this section, I'll cover a few additional tips that my colleagues and I have found helpful in designing and delivering programs that will have the desired impact.

## Define a few specific and attainable learning goals

Don't try to teach too much or require too much to be learned and applied. It's better to reinforce a few key lessons that can be absorbed and remembered than to saturate your participants with a torrent of details that will be quickly forgotten. In other words, make sure each lesson has just a few key themes. The simpler and clearer the message, the easier it will be for people to understand and retrieve when needed. To pick up a phrase from earlier in the book, "What will be different?" What behaviors concern you now that you want to see disappear? What existing behaviors do you want to see more of? What new behaviors should take the places of old norms?

As just discussed, for example, telling people they must act with integrity is a broad statement of purpose. Telling them *not to lie, fabricate information, or cover up problems* gives them behaviors they can understand and consistently apply. If left open to too much interpretation, one person could behave in a way they think is fine but others believe violates the value.

## Don't overly legalize the content

I have often heard clients say that behavioral initiatives that focus on or include legal subjects are slowed because content has to be vetted by lawyers. I understand this, and it is important that a legal review process occurs. But what often happens is that the content ends up being legally accurate but incomprehensible or numbingly boring to the student. The quest for legally perfect framing can so monopolize review processes that the issue of impact and processes to reinforce learning are overlooked completely.

Though unstated, another aspect of this policy has been "we don't want anyone except a few experts discussing these topics. We can't chance our people messing up and saying or doing something that creates liability." That's an outmoded and non-productive way of looking at risk. I've been reading cases for nearly 40 years and have yet to find one where an organization lost a claim because a non-lawyer leader or manager tried too hard to communicate the organization's commitment to lawful, ethical, or inclusive conduct. Yet I can remember many examples where initiatives died because, after the class, frontline leaders failed to apply or talk about them or demonstrate their importance.

In sum, don't confuse what lawyers have to know to do their job well with what everyone needs to know to conform with civil treatment values. These are two audiences with very different needs. Learning on compliance and related topics is not intended to train lawyers. It's intended to convey information that can be easily absorbed and applied on the job and to give participants a sense of key issues and when to get help if they are not sure what to do.

The greatest risk is that key principles won't be broadly applied, not that some manager will innocently misstate an obscure legal requirement.

## Use respected messengers

The message won't be respected if the messenger does not have credence with the audience. That holds true for everyone from the leaders setting the tone and holding people accountable to the educators involved in training or instruction.

Leaders will have credibility if their actions demonstrate that the topic is important to them personally and to the organization, as I've discussed elsewhere.

Educators have credibility if they have the right professional credentials and/or the trust and respect of the learners. When I deliver training at an organization, my credibility initially comes from my professional background and being an expert on the subject being taught. Ultimately, however, how I deliver information determines whether that initial credibility builds or diminishes.

# Reinforce, Reinforce, Reinforce

What differentiates a one-and-done education event with minimal impact from a learning journey that creates lasting change is what happens after the class when people return to their jobs. My belief is that the best post-event reinforcement comes in many small steps, in multiple formats and venues. Formal reinforcement can help but is far less effective when it comes to developing new norms. What is far more effective is when reinforcement becomes organic. Here are three ways to make that happen:

## 1. Have leaders become on-the-job teachers

One of my favorite instructional methods is to have leaders become coaches and teachers back on the job. Requiring them to teach others forces them to learn and understand the concepts and new behaviors, if for no other reason than they don't want to embarrass themselves in front of their employees or be viewed as a hypocrite. And by "teaching" I don't mean having them walk through a manual. I mean talking about what the ideas mean in practical everyday life, helping to answer questions, and reinforcing key principles in actual daily situations. I mean teaching by modeling civil treatment behaviors.

Since it's easy for people to forget danger signals and stay trapped in old ways of doing business, leaders should also provide periodic reminders about key risks or main issues addressed in the training. Those reminders can be formal, in the form of mini-exercises or simulations, or, more importantly, informal comments woven into routine conversations about key practices. Or perhaps the leader can use demonstrations, discuss actual cases (especially current events), or even create simulated problems in staff meetings to show how to apply key skills.

Having leaders demonstrate and reinforce skills increases the odds they will learn and apply the skills themselves and become powerful role models for the rest of the organization.

---

### Anti-role models as powerful teachers

In the early '90s, I worked with a leader in a nuclear power plant. He came into a meeting with his arms folded and his face grimly set. He thought what we were teaching was "political correctness" and not worth listening to—and he had the courage to say it. He admitted he had engaged in a lot of the behaviors that needed to be changed. We spent some time with him and focused on getting him to look at the impact of his conduct. He got it and after several days said he saw things in a new light.

This "student" became one of the most effective teachers in this organization. He could say, "I get it. I once did all these things. But I can change. If I get it and if I can change, then so can you. And that's what we've all got to do—starting with me." He then modeled and taught the skills on the job and he became a great advocate.

---

## 2. Allow for peer-to-peer exchanges and on-the-job practice

I listened to our instructor explaining how our new software package will work. I was excited to learn and use this tool—it would ease communication and improve how my company did business. There was a lot to absorb.

I followed the presentation closely, watching screen after screen of instruction. The instructor was very good. But certain processes just did not, excuse the pun, compute for me. I got lost in a flood of new operations. Luckily, my executive assistant sat next to me. At a couple of key places, she moved over to my laptop and showed me the right commands. She knew exactly how to explain what the instructor said in terms that related to our application.

Then I went on the road for a few weeks, and the next time I sat in front of the computer, my mind was a complete blank because I hadn't had a chance to use the new software immediately. So I got a quick refresher, then practiced and applied what I had learned. After that, I knew how to use the software (at least the key functions I needed). I also learned that to keep my knowledge alive I would have to use the program frequently so I would learn and remember key functions. I did that daily for a few weeks and now what I need to use is automatic.

The lesson: while complex skills should be introduced by knowledgeable instructors, we often learn best from people who are learning and dealing with the same problems, challenges, and issues that we are. Co-workers who have been through similar experiences and learning curves can be great instructors, whether in the classroom or on the job. That's true whether the topic is new software commands or how to change the workplace to make it more civil, inclusive, and productive.

When people are learning new values, complex ideas, or new skills they will have questions. They need to practice new behaviors, and most will need help when doing so. Perhaps you disagree with or don't understand a concept—and who better to help you translate ideas to your situation than someone who has already worked through the same questions? In that way, colleagues are often your best tutors. They're the ones who can give you a different perspective, challenge your assumptions, or explain an issue in a way that is specific to the work you do (something even the most talented instructors often fail to do). And they can prove that new behaviors can be learned and applied if they have gone through the same process and made the same adjustments themselves.

## 3. Weave civil treatment into other communications

One point made in Chapter 3 was that behavior, civil and uncivil, is a key aspect of almost everything an organization does. Another way to reinforce the importance of civility, therefore, is to make sure you regularly and explicitly address behavioral goals and standards in conjunction with other topics that have a behavioral component. For example, leaders could bring up the idea of "welcoming concerns" or "acting professionally" when discussing everything from inclusion and compliance to safety, quality control, customer service, teamwork, accounting, or countless other topics. That way, employees will stop seeing civility and behavior as something separate from their daily work and instead understand how it affects the overall performance of themselves, their work unit, and the organization as a whole.

## Summary: Turning Learning into Action

E-learning, webcasts, multiple classes, and even emails, to a degree, can communicate lessons about key points and achieve positive results. Then the company just needs to put in the equivalent of a speed trap so that people will know if they have violated the policy. This is how many compliance training programs work. We give participants the standards, document receipt, and call it a day. Then, if key rules are breached, offenders "pay the price." We blame the lapse on errant participants. This process may limit organizational fines and sanctions, but it does not change behavior and does not help foster civil treatment behaviors or create enduring cultural change.

But to shift behaviors, you need a far more robust approach to learning and education. As you may have detected, the points I make in this chapter are rooted in basic adult learning strategies, which are built around the need for participants to recognize for themselves *why* they have to change and quickly reach a point of applying the lessons on the job. When you think this way, you will lean towards using methods that require learners to identify a problem, think through solutions, then apply the principles you're trying to teach.

Unfortunately, we all know that leaders and employees alike are under great pressure to produce these days. The pressure to get "real work" done, the conceptual resistance many people will have to the subject, and their lack of comfort in behaving in new ways in front of their peers all contribute to some high barriers to learning that is converted into action. Because of those pressures, organizations too often take the easy path by loading people up with rule after rule and densely written technical information using traditional education methods that essentially spoon feed information to participants. This approach has never helped anyone change long-standing and comfortable habits that, in their view, have made them successful.

The omnipresence of workplace distractions makes it imperative that your educational efforts engage employees in the learning and go beyond abstraction to give them skills they can use back on the job. You must provide a context for what is being taught in terms of what really happens in the workplace, what the roadblocks are to handling situations effectively, and possible strategies for dealing with them. That is the best way to provide a good foundation for changing behavior.

CHAPTER 9

# Choosing the Right Delivery Methods

The principles of shaping an initiative that will not just educate your workforce but lead to behavior change were covered in the previous chapter. From an implementation standpoint, the challenge is finding the right delivery approaches for meeting the goals; approaches must balance effectiveness against resource availability. Modern learning technologies have a role to play but, as with any learning methodology, must be used with an understanding of the purpose and value being sought, as well as the pluses and minuses of available delivery options. This chapter talks about two of the methodology decisions you'll face that will have a big impact on the overall effectiveness of your initiative:

1) Whether to use online or in-person instructions

2) Whether to make the educational experience available just-in-time (JIT) or as part of preparatory training

## The Strengths of In-Person Training

I remember one instance where an executive was attending my in-house class on workplace responsibilities. At first, he looked me in the eye, spoke up, and listened to those around him. But something changed when we started talking about a leader's responsibility to get help from human resources or other representatives when a harassment claim has been made. For many leaders, even today, this a challenging concept, especially, as in this instance, if the person complaining is a male employee who was the recipient of sexual advances launched by a female coworker and the employee wanted the matter to remain confidential (between him and his manager).

That's when this executive folded his arms, frowned at the ceiling, shook his head left and right, and pushed his body back in his chair. I realized he had reached a point where his conceptual resistance took over, and I was facing one of the toughest learning problems dealing with ethical, legal, and related issues. Often it's this underlying disagreement that causes people not to apply what they have been taught, to conclude that the lessons they are supposed to be learning are impractical or against their own values or leadership instincts.

Knowing that conceptual resistance never disappears unless challenged, I asked the executive how he would handle this situation so he could openly discuss his opinion. Here's what he said:

> *"In this kind of situation, I'm not going to get help, and I'm not going to take it further. The guy in your hypothetical is a wimp if he can't handle this. He ought to be able to handle a woman hitting on him. That's all there is to say about it. Anything else makes no sense and is just going to cause us big trouble for no reason."*

His candid answer gave me the chance to ask him other questions to illustrate what could happen if he ignored knowledge of a potential violation of organizational policy and maybe the law. His colleagues in the room also spoke up, giving him the opportunity to hear how they viewed the problem. They told him he had to act and why the organization and everyone involved could be harmed if he didn't. Ultimately, he said he saw a side to the problem he hadn't recognized. (I suspect others in the room may have felt the same way he did but had chosen to keep quiet. They also had the chance to learn from his and the class's comments.)

This personal interaction with me and especially with his fellow students helped this executive understand why he had to change his behavior. And it's that kind of conversation that could not happen with an online course, even one that is taught with a live instructor via a webcast or more enhanced virtual learning methods. Thus, despite the push for a technological educational experience, there are many reasons why live classrooms have survived since Socrates, if not before.

My friend Phil Weis agrees with me. He's a senior in-house employment attorney in the pharmaceutical industry. Phil, who has worked with employment training issues for many years, told me recently, "I'm a strong proponent of classroom learning. If you can have people's full and undivided attention, in a group setting, with no distractions, there's no better way to teach adults. People get a chance to learn not just from the instructor but from each other. If one person speaks up about an aha moment, the whole class can have an aha moment. If someone is puzzled and asks a question, other people with the same question can get an answer. And if you have them sitting at tables where they can face each other and engage in discussion, so much the better."

However, he added, there is a caveat: to take advantage of that situation, the organization has to have instructors who can deliver the content and lead discussions with energy, passion, honesty, and integrity. "I've been in front of some professional facilitators who didn't have their heart in what they were teaching. You could tell by the way they deflected questions and wouldn't stray from the agenda," Phil said. "There's a difference between simply delivering the content and getting the job done. A well-designed, interactive, online program can be a better choice than being in a classroom with an uninspiring instructor." And I would add the same holds true for deliveries presented by instructors who aren't seen as credible to participants.

If your organization can commit to creating great experiences, engaging classroom learning is often the preferred mode in situations where:

- The lessons being taught are of high strategic value to the organization and their application can have long-term critical significance to business success.

- The principles being taught are likely to generate conceptual resistance (as behavioral issues are). As Chapter 5 discussed, when people misbehave, it's generally not due to a lack of information; it's due to a decision to ignore or purposely violate key standards. As we just saw, in a classroom there's an opportunity to challenge willful denial via dialogue and the responses of other participants. With any one-way delivery of information—whether classroom lecture or online module—this opportunity to challenge such assumptions and how they really may and do play out doesn't exist.

- Learning can be enhanced by discussions between students. While technology does allow for discussion groups among remote participants, there's nothing like listening to another learner sitting right next to you, speaking right to you, and telling you why he or she disagrees with your point of view.

- It's important to explore nuance, e.g., where individual questions will relate to special situations that need to be analyzed and factual differences matter. In a live class, an experienced instructor with a few back-and-forth questions can illustrate how different situations require different approaches.

- The organization's commitment and credibility are part of the message. Nothing beats having a leader speak directly to his or her audience and convincingly say a particular topic and principle are important and invite tough questions face to face. Pre-recorded or unidirectional learning doesn't allow that.

- The teaching focuses on skills involving interpersonal communication and problem solving based on how other people react. It's easy to explain to someone how to communicate a difficult subject. But in any situation where responses can vary, a back-and-forth exchange between the instructor and the audience is necessary.

---

**A practical option:**
**Leveraging recordings of live sessions**

Phil Weis's company once asked him to do a series of webcasts that needed to reach hundreds of field personnel. Phil ended up doing a series of live, unscripted webcasts for 50 people at a time. Since it was live, the webcast had many of the advantages of classroom training: for example, people could ask questions and get answers, and listen to comments and questions from others.

Phil did six of these webcasts and recorded the final one, which was watched by about 100 people who couldn't participate in the live webcasts.

"There comes a point of diminishing returns for the live sessions," said Phil. "It wasn't a good use of my time to keep trying to schedule additional sessions. This way, we reached the majority of people in a reasonably interactive format, and could reach everyone else with the recording."

---

# The Role of Online Learning

It's clear that many organizations just don't have the time for traditional classroom training for all employees, or they may have widely dispersed audiences, which makes live instruction impractical. For some audiences and topics, in-class deliveries are useful and necessary. For many others, it isn't practical, which leaves organizations turning to various forms of online training. Generally, these fall into two categories:

- **Virtual instructor-led synchronous training** (often referred to as VILT): At a designated time, a live instructor is joined by participants in real time. The amount of interaction can vary widely, from submitting questions in a chat window to fully functional audio and video sharing (everyone can see and interact with everyone else).

- **Asynchronous training**: There is a packaged module that participants watch at a time of their choosing.

Both of these delivery methods have positives and negatives. Synchronous training can have an impact comparable to a live classroom experience if done properly and also is often more time- and cost-effective, but does have some important logistical challenges and requirements (see sidebar, next page). Asynchronous online training can reach huge numbers of people quickly without pulling them from their jobs and provide easy access to useful information at the learner's convenience rather than the instructor's. But participants do not have a chance to ask questions of the instructor or benefit from the discussions of others taking the class, which are often critical to overcoming conceptual resistance.

Either way, delivering great content, while vital, by itself is not enough to create a true learning experience when complex issues are involved. That's true no matter what the format: in-class, live webinars, or online packaged modules.

Mark Edmundson, a distinguished professor at the University of Virginia, points to a problem with online lecture learning when it's viewed as the *only* or even *primary* means of instruction: usually, there is no meaningful interaction between the teacher and students. Instead, the teacher lectures and it's assumed that invisible students will

## VILT done right

My colleagues and I have seen a boom in the interest in VILT (virtual instructor-led training) recently. Since VILT is another form of adult instruction, it needs to be designed with the same care you would use for any other educational experience (as discussed in Chapter 8)—plus be developed with an eye towards the technical challenges. You can't, for instance, simply take a live class and deliver it in front of a camera. To be most effective with VILT, it's important to:

**Tip 1: Think in tandem about the content and how you will use the virtual medium to get the message across.** You will not be able to directly transfer an 8-hour classroom experience to a virtual platform. Studies show the maximum viable attention span of any virtual session is about 90 minutes to 2 hours. In the world of the six-second Vine video, you will also have to be willing to truncate your message down to the most salient points (less is more) and change up interactivity every two to three minutes to maintain interest.

**Tip 2: Plan production very carefully.** Successful virtual sessions require a very high level of collaboration between all the players—the facilitator, the producer, IT or the stakeholder who owns your virtual platform, the subject matter expert, and the stakeholder who is requesting the training for his or her employees.

**Tip 3: Make sure the instructor is comfortable with the technology.** Chapter 8 talked about the importance of using "respected messengers," and the same holds true here. But those messengers also need to be competent in the technology and experienced as online presenters or the effort will be wasted.

**Tip 4: Think about your broadcast as a live television event and throw in a bit of the unexpected.** Try to incorporate an appropriate participant challenge with a game-show theme, engage a surprise guest speaker, broadcast tasteful music to support a theme, etc., to change things up at unexpected times throughout the experience.

magically absorb information. Edmundson's point is that there is no dialogue, which is what often furthers learning: teachers can't respond to the needs of the students and the students can't ask questions or discuss what they've learned with one another.

With online learning, there are other barriers to learning that must be addressed. Though it is convenient and flexible, people often look on it as a chore and use the time to multitask in the extreme. They won't absorb key content and will miss what they are supposed to learn. Further, often there is no mention of the concepts back on the job, no discussion by their manager. Also, during a live class, the instructor can ask the learners to commit to specific actions, and their peers are there to witness it! That peer reinforcement doesn't happen with most online learning.

Additionally, some people—especially leaders in senior roles—have been known to get aides, assistants, or others to take courses for them. These leaders learn nothing and, even worse, their actions say to others that neither content nor integrity matters.

E-learning initiatives, whether VILT or prepackaged modules, need to change these patterns. As discussed earlier, they must make sure that leaders send the right messages before and after the training, and help develop ways for leaders to reinforce the concepts on the job. All of this must be planned and not left to chance.

Ultimately, as Phil Weis said to me, the real issue is what constitutes effective training. All three major formats—classroom, webcasts, and online—can deliver if the execution is done well.

I'll take Phil's point one step further: what's really important is not what participants are taught; it's what they do that is most important. Whether your learning is delivered in person or online, it must reach your resistant learners in order to have a long-term impact. We should be considering how to make sure that all of our learning methods address conceptual resistance if we want our investment in education and talent to yield the best results, which is to prevent, detect, and correct problems before they lead to workplace disasters.

## Proactive vs. JIT Learning

There's a trend these days to make much training "just in time" (JIT), meaning people are educated on a particular concept, tool, or method when they have an immediate need to apply it. Today, JIT takes two forms: a trainer offers a short, targeted course to people who have encountered a problem or have a specific need; or any employee can access specific training modules (online or through dedicated portals) whenever they need it, at a time of their choosing.

The principle is sound: people are more likely to remember a lesson when they have a clear need and get to use a new skill or tool or methodology immediately. All of us tend to learn best when we have a need to solve a current problem—that way, there is a clear purpose to the learning and finding a solution matters to us. For that reason, JIT training is an effective approach as long as you know how and when to use it.

There are some limitations with using JIT training (whether via trainer or online module) to do the initial instruction around civility, compliance, discrimination, etc. That's because a JIT model is built around these underlying assumptions:

1) An important, specific issue will arise.

2) The person will appreciate its significance.

3) The person will realize that help is available to them.

4) The person will have immediate access to the trainer-led course or online module that deals with the issue.

These assumptions often do not hold true when it comes to the complex issues regarding workplace behavior.

First, you don't know when an issue may arise. If people have not received prior training, they may not know what help is available for the issue they have encountered, even if they were once told about available sessions. If the JIT module is used as reinforcement of principles or skills taught in a course, you can't expect people to remember that reinforcement is available if it's been weeks or months since they went through the learning experience.

Second, the person may not recognize the issue soon enough. That is, they don't label the situation as a "civil treatment" issue until after the fact.

Third, having information, wisdom, and knowledge available just in time won't help if the targeted end user doesn't see the urgency in accessing it, or if they don't know what's available to them or how to get to it.

Lastly, the range of potential uncivil behaviors is so broad that you can't possibly prepare modules on every topic.

Because of these issues, you have to be judicious in how you use JIT learning. If you want it available as the primary mode of learning, then consider using teaching partners spread throughout your organization who can help people recognize that a problem has arisen and that a learning program is available to help them, and be on hand to deliver the training without too much delay.

Keep in mind that one of the biggest issues with creating a more civil workplace is dealing with resistant learners (people who don't recognize that what they're doing is a problem and see no reason to change). Obviously, people with that mentality are unlikely to seek out JIT modules you have—providing one more reason why a JIT approach may not be successful if it is your sole or even primary form of instruction.

That's why you will have to be proactive in reminding people that help is available and make sure they know what topics are covered and how they can access the trainers or online modules. Your goal is to make it likely that employees will connect something they see or experience in the workplace with a module you have available, and make it easy for them to find what they need in terms of instruction or refreshers.

Also, whenever possible, anticipate issues and be proactive in alerting people to the availability of reminder modules. For example, nowadays, holiday parties where alcohol is served are more risky than they used to be because (1) sensibilities are more cautious than in the past, (2) missteps can be indelibly captured via video or audio recordings, (3) the evidence can quickly go viral. Pre-holiday, some organizations are sending out a pop quiz or hypothetical scenarios to alert leaders of potential issues at holiday time and remind them where to find tools they can use to prevent problems or deal with them if they start to arise at such events.

# Summary:
# Effective Delivery for Effective Learning

As we continue to adopt stunning new technologies that allow us to spread information broadly and get people to take tests and answer problems demonstrating they understand the key concepts, we need to keep in mind the necessity of addressing areas of complexity, confusion, and even conceptual resistance. That's why I want to offer a word of caution about going strictly to online and/or just-in-time training. While both of those practices have their place in the instructional toolbox, they also have limitations when it comes to behavioral change. If you choose to use these approaches, make sure that you provide a context for the training so people understand how they fit in with your other educational efforts.

# Education in Context

As I hope you realize now, the purpose of education in a civil treatment effort is much broader than defending or preventing lawsuits. It is to change behavior that, if unaddressed, can have a widespread negative impact on productivity and other business metrics and potentially lead to legal claims. For that, you need to find ways to make sure that people truly learn what you are trying to teach and will act differently in the workplace.

I believe in the value and use of formal education in all its many formats (online, in person, etc.). And I urge you to carefully consider all the factors that go into developing an engaging learning experience. There is no single answer to the "best" educational approach regarding what specifically is taught and what delivery method is used (live instructor, in-house or external trainers, online learning, etc.), no single method that is right or wrong in and of itself.

The proper lens for evaluating learning strategies is to think about what your organization is doing to either foster or impede learner motivation. Put another way, what is your organization doing or not doing to motivate people to learn about important topics and change their behavior? Table A (next page) has some questions that will help you get started evaluating what you are already doing right and what may need improving.

**Table A: How Effective Is Your Educational Approach?**

| | True | False |
|---|---|---|
| We require completion or attendance by all employees (leaders included). | | |
| We require leaders to discuss key messages informally and formally, on a regular basis. | | |
| We reinforce learning with short reminders frequently to supplement what's taught. | | |
| We link learning to job performance so what we require is as clear as a sales quota, a safety requirement, or quality standard. | | |
| We make sure that what we teach is:<br>• linked to our values and how we work together.<br>• not presented solely as a matter of legal compliance and or avoiding/defending lawsuits. | | |
| We teach a combination of information and behaviorally based skills. As part of learning, skills are practiced. | | |

You won't be graded on this quiz, but based on the discussion in this chapter and previous chapters, it should be clear that the ideal is having 100% "True" answers. That would indicate you're using a mix of strategies to make sure that messages are communicated repeatedly and employees have multiple ways to test out and explore the behavioral changes you're requesting. That's the way to have a lasting impact on ethics and civil treatment in your workplace.

At this point, I feel compelled to reiterate that formal education is just one component of a successful civil treatment initiative. For important subjects where behavioral change is necessary and especially where people must change long-standing habits (behaviors that come naturally to them), there are many other ingredients, such as direct leadership support and persuasion through behavioral modeling. Even the best training can't take the place of daily modeling and reinforcement, which I've alluded to before and will discuss in more detail in Part III.

# Part III

# Make It Work

# Speaking with Actions

A colleague and I once visited the headquarters of a nationally known organization. The leadership team had asked us to help them deal with problems they were having with several key people whose behavior had become highly disruptive and was harming morale. (If I sound like a broken record, it's because this particular issue comes up frequently!)

The first thing the organization's leaders did was show us around their brand-new buildings—the result of years of planning and $250 million in fundraising. The facilities had the latest and greatest equipment, and the leaders were justifiably proud of what this investment would mean in terms of serving customers and improving the bottom line.

Yet later in the day when we got around to talking about the reason for my team's visit, the leaders were much more tentative. They were hesitant in describing the behaviors they wanted to see changed and weren't sure what, if any, actions to take for fear of insulting the key players.

These senior leaders had made a huge investment of their own time and the organization's budget to make sure they had the best facilities. They were eloquent in detailing how new buildings and state-of-the-art equipment could help them become more efficient and improve service. Yet they had not invested any time and energy in addressing improper behaviors; they had not defined the impact that uncivil behavior could have on the bottom line and other important indicators of success.

I found it ironic that this organization had built a world-class facility but had not built an equally world-class professional environment where employees could do their best work. They had willingly invested millions in new equipment, which can become obsolete, but not in the kinds of organizational improvements that would have (a) cost less than the equipment, (b) had just as big if not a bigger positive impact, and (c) potentially lasted longer than the equipment, if done correctly. Had these leaders spent just a fraction of their investment on learning how to better manage behavior, they could have generated equally dramatic improvements in productivity and other business measures while also resolving problems promptly and reducing compliance and legal risks.

In some respects, a civil treatment initiative can be extremely challenging to implement. For one thing, there are the usual complications of developing an organization-wide rollout. For another, you have to try to convince *every person* in your organization to change their own behavior (knowing that you'll never be 100% successful), either so they recognize and stop doing things that are now unacceptable or feel comfortable speaking up if they observe unacceptable behaviors. You have to encompass everything from outright illegal to subtle behaviors under the same umbrella.

I won't attempt to cover all the basics of change management here—obviously, it would require a separate book to cover everything that has to be planned (sequencing, messaging, how to reach different audiences, timing, etc.). Instead, the following chapters focus on leverage points that have the biggest impact on whether an initiative will succeed and endure.

# CHAPTER 10

# Laying the Foundation

Let's remember the ultimate goal here. Organizations benefit when they make the most of their human capital, and civil treatment is a means to accomplish that end. It allows an organization to create a workplace where employees:

- Can concentrate and perform at their best; they are not distracted by behaviors that hinder creativity, stifle contributions, or make them feel unwelcome.

- Care about their work and their employer.

- Act in line with basic codes of conduct and rules.

- Speak up to share their ideas and concerns.

- Trust that they and others in the organization can work out problems quickly and effectively.

- Are treated based on their merit, accomplishment, skills, and talents.

In their eagerness to achieve these goals, leaders who are committed to creating behavioral changes may plunge right into tactical issues. They try to tackle the *how* before they figure out the *what* and *why* or *where* they want to end up. They start thinking about how to reach audiences in terms of getting messages out before figuring out what the messages are and how to translate those messages for different audiences. They worry about whether to use online learning or class-room experiences before thinking through what it is that they want to actually change. That is a serious, common, and costly mistake. While all of these issues are important, they should be reserved for the point in the process where the organization knows exactly what it is going to implement, the desired behavioral outcomes it wants to create, and how it intends to sustain its initiative and implementation.

Rather than rushing into the tactics of communication and education, take the time to lay a solid foundation. Make sure you are clear about your aim (the vision for the future and the values needed to support that vision) and what changes you need to see before thinking about how to make the changes happen. Here are three pieces of that foundation:

1) Build a unified front driven by executive ownership

2) Identify specific behavioral concerns

3) Develop a solid business case

# 1) Build a Unified Front Driven by Executive Ownership

As I discussed in Chapter 3, organizations traditionally view behavioral issues—inclusion, diversity, discrimination, etc.—as separate fiefdoms. So naturally they treat any efforts in these areas as separate initiatives, usually delegating the design and rollout to human resources, compliance, and/or the legal department. The more effective approach is to unite all behavior issues under one umbrella, led at the executive level and championed within all departments.

Why this approach? As I talked about in Chapter 3, you'll have a harder row to hoe if your HR department is seen as initiating, driving, and leading the effort to make improvements in behavior. HR initiatives, rightly or wrongly, are often discounted by employees, labeled as check-the-box exercises (something they have to do to meet a requirement but that is of little value to them) or a "feel good" activity (something that may provide a temporary boost in morale but has no significance for ongoing work).

Also, isolating civil treatment as an HR initiative runs counter to the goals of the effort, which are to improve overall business performance, maximize teamwork everywhere, make it easier for all employees to contribute, and avoid illegal behaviors (and lawsuits). These broad goals mean you have to work to prevent as many uncivil behaviors as possible, not just those that violate any specific legal area (harassment, compliance, discrimination, etc.).

Remember the first component of the mantra for Chapter 7, *Make it Matter*. Civil treatment must matter to *everyone*—leaders, middle management, and frontline employees alike—or it will not succeed. It is critical, therefore, to have a broad-based implementation team. The mode and style of communication must convey as much information as the actual message and demonstrate the initiative is about business performance. That way, the supporters outside of HR and related fields can give credence to the fact that the goal is operational excellence.

## 2) Identify Specific Behavioral Concerns

The potential reach and success of a civil treatment effort is determined at the outset by how well you convince your organization's leaders that paying attention to the umbrella of civility issues is a business necessity, not a nicety. Developing a compelling business case to gain their support is the topic of the next section. In this section, I want to focus on one of the most important aspects of that business case: describing specifically the behaviors that do (or should) concern leaders and how they will be addressed by the initiative.

Generally, the kinds of behaviors that should come under scrutiny fall into the following categories:

- Behaviors that discourage people from speaking up about concerns.

- Behaviors that are unsafe, that represent a risk of harm to employees, customers, property, or the community.

- Behaviors that unconsciously skew HR decisions (around hiring, promotion, disciplinary actions, etc.).

- Behaviors that have the potential to create overt legal risk around compliance or discrimination, for example. This could include racial, sexual, religious, age, and ethnic jokes, comments and banter—spoken, emailed, or however communicated.

- Behaviors that create an unwelcoming and hostile environment, such as screaming, yelling, or calling other people names in public or private settings. This includes body language, gestures, and tone of voice that communicate disdain. (By the way, these non-verbals can be specifically defined: think about how a sneer, a sarcastic inflection, a dismissive gesture, or lack of eye contact can affect how you receive messages.)

- Behaviors that violate the organization's values, such as lying or fabricating information in any context.

- Behaviors that distract people from focusing and concentrating on their daily tasks and responsibilities.

There are many ways that companies can find out which of these behaviors are an issue for them. For example, they can review records of employee concerns and hotline reports to see if there are any common themes, look at the results of engagement surveys, or if needed, prepare targeted surveys to get an anecdotal sense of what is occurring in terms of employee and leader behaviors, actions, and concerns. If there are known areas of trouble or concern (such as the one surgery department in Hospital X), then doing face-to-face interviews with a sample of employees at all levels can be very effective at providing the kinds of information you need to set as priorities for change.

# 3) Develop a Solid Business Case

Not that long ago, simply equating an initiative to lowering legal risks or regulated issues would carry the day. Selling civil treatment nowadays is more challenging; even if the issue is trying to lower legal risk, the mentality is often "do the least we can" not "what's the best we can do to minimize risk now and into the future."

Therefore, if you are talking to a leader considering an initiative to build or enhance standards of civility, ethics, and inclusion, here are the questions he or she will probably ask you: "Why should we do this?" … "Will this work?" … "How can you prove it?" … "What's the cost?" … and "What's the payoff for me, my department, and the organization?" You need to be able to provide answers that the leader will find compelling and believable, to provide answers that will convince your leaders that civil treatment is a necessity because of its hard-line impact on the business, not just a nice-to-have that will make some people feel better. (This is another reason why the initiative can't be seen as something solely or primarily championed by HR—almost automatically that labels the effort as "nice" instead of "necessary.")

For leaders who already have to balance competing business needs and anyone in your organization who is tied to the old, accepted ways of behavior, you need to provide them with a powerful reason to make an enduring change. That "powerful reason" is the business case you will compile. There has to be a clear sense of the business benefits that will accrue from long-term change. If there is not an understanding that working on civil treatment is important to the business, to employees, and to leaders personally, then there is no reason to move forward.

Assuming that you have identified specific behaviors of concern (the previous step), the business case will explain:

1) The costs of doing nothing (the harm done to the organization by tolerating the current state).

2) The benefits from behavioral change (avoiding negatives and creating positives).

3) The likely cost of taking action.

When done effectively, these three ingredients will lead your executives to several key conclusions: "Yes, culture change is needed"; "I

---

### Speak to your audience

The business case you develop must be made in terms of *your* organization, not any other organization's. To establish credibility, it's helpful to present examples, successes, references, and an established methodology that have been demonstrated to work through implementation at other organizations.

But you can't *only* say, "We're doing this because Acme had great results." It is too easy for people to dismiss the need for change if all they hear are examples from other organizations. It is more powerful to prove the case using stories, examples, and goals from *your* organization. People will connect most with lessons pertaining to their work, employers, and careers rather than what has happened somewhere else.

The goal here is similar to a technique that nonprofits use to persuade potential donors by getting them to focus on a single person's experience—that is much more powerful than a generic statement like "50 people have suffered." The same holds true in terms of using real life anecdotes from your organization as opposed to industry statistics alone to prove workplace points.

understand the outcomes"; and "It's all worth it." Let's see how you can make those happen.

## Understand the cost of doing nothing

Put another way, this is the cost to your organization of the uncivil behaviors of concern (identified in the previous step). I've been through the many costs of uncivil behavior in previous chapters, but as a visual recap you just need to look at the behavioral triangle (see Figure 12) and think about how all of these harm your organization.

### Figure 12: The Uncivil Triangle

The familiar Hospital X story illustrates the kind of tally you should do here. For them, the cost of doing nothing about the badly behaving surgeons includes:

- Increased potential that staff will make a mistake or fail to raise a concern—which could directly and potentially fatally affect patients.

- Constant distraction and increased stress on all associated staff (nurses, pharmacists, anesthesiologists, technicians, etc.).

- Increased turnover.

- Difficulty in attracting additional top professionals.

## Identify the benefits of change

Benefits from creating a more civil workplace environment come in two forms: (1) Minimizing the presence of uncivil behaviors and all the negative impact they have, and (2) Creating positive behaviors that improve productivity, creativity, recruitment, retention, and loyalty. It's one thing to eliminate a negative but to realize a positive at the same time is a powerful incentive (see Figure 13).

### Figure 13: Cumulative Benefits of Civil Treatment

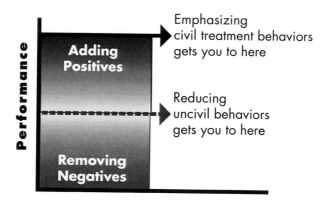

To use a sports analogy, it's as if a visiting football team is about to score a touchdown but the home team intercepts a pass in the end zone and returns it the full length of the field to score. Whereas the home team could have been down by 7 points, it is now up by 7 points—a 14 point swing!

Minimizing uncivil behaviors is like the interception: it prevents you from being down 7 points. Creating a more civil workplace is like the run down the field and subsequent score, which puts you ahead by 7 points.

---

### Highlighting negatives that outweigh positives

In many situations, the business case has to explain why the supposed benefits of tolerated behavior are not as big as the costs of those behaviors. As discussed earlier, many organizations have unwritten special rules for big shots, rainmakers, and other types of stellar performers. They put up with bad behavior from those players because they think whatever those people bring—prestige, dollars, results—is worth the cost. But once they start paying attention to *all* the costs of the uncivil behaviors, they realize that perhaps the price is too high. When talking to people in your organization, ideally you would draw on specific examples of how the behaviors have harmed it.

---

## Tally the likely costs of taking action

No evaluation is complete until you counterbalance benefits with the cost. Admittedly, changing behavior is essentially a change in culture, and therefore is not an insignificant undertaking. There will need to be an initial investment in training that reaches all corners of the organization, plus some effort to reinforce and sustain behaviors.

But here's good news: those costs are often relatively minor compared with other expenses, and if you're successful, the cost of sustaining the changes will drop dramatically. Think of it this way: you didn't invest a cent in *creating* bad behaviors; you didn't host courses on "how to be a jerk" or "simple ways to undermine compliance" or "sexual harassment 101." The bad stuff was reinforced by a culture of tolerance or indifference. Once new norms and behaviors take root, they will become routine and automatically reinforced the same way. That is what culture change is all about. Once the process starts and is rewarded and copied, it works by itself. What we are trying to do is to change the process and use the same kind of reinforcement that got behavior off track to bring it back to where it should be.

In short, anticipate a significant initial investment but quickly reducing costs if you are successful in shifting behavior.

## Summary: Pulling It All Together

The advice in this chapter amounts to building a case that makes sense to anyone and everyone you need to convince to support your civil treatment initiative. Your business case should state what your organization wants to achieve and why that is important, and explain how civil treatment helps you make the most of your talents and resources. Tie the changes into the good results for individuals, other employees, the organization as a whole, and likely your customers or community.

With the three components in place—a unified front focused on specific behavioral concerns, bolstered by a solid business case—you are ready to tackle the design and rollout of an implementation.

*Dr. Keith Miller is the president of Greenville Technical College in Greenville, S.C. The college has four campuses serving over 13,000 students, with nearly 800 academic staff. His work with the leadership team at GTC is an example of how to engage leaders in establishing and maintaining the change.*

CASE 4: GREENVILLE TECHNICAL COLLEGE

# From the Top Down

Like a lot of organizations in both private business and academia, Greenville Technical College (GTC) has had difficulties with diversity in the past. "We made some progress over the past decade, but about two or three years ago we started having some serious discussions about how we could improve diversity," said Dr. Keith Miller, president of the college. Those discussions quickly evolved to a point where college leaders realized they wanted training and awareness on something broader than just diversity.

"In a way, the path we ultimately took was a little selfish on my part," said Keith. "It was my firm belief that everybody is here on this campus for a reason, that every person can bring expertise to the table. And it is my responsibility—the responsibility of leadership—to make sure we create an environment that taps into all the skills and knowledge available to us. I wanted to find some tools that would help us do that. If I didn't, then all the expertise out there would be inaccessible to my organization."

Combining the need to improve diversity and inclusion with Keith's view of management's responsibility drove GTC to take the behavioral approach that I label "civil treatment" to address their needs.

"Anytime you have more than one person in an organization, you will have personnel issues," said Keith. "Some of them are difficult to deal with. We recognize at Greenville Tech that there is a civil way to deal with even the difficult things, and how we deal with them contributes to creating the environment we want to have."

The formal training phase of the initiative started with Keith's cabinet, which included vice presidents and other administrators who report directly to him. The management team was the second group to get trained, and only then was the training rolled out to the rest of the employee community. "We wanted to make sure that employees knew that this training wasn't just for them. It had to be about management, too," said Keith.

Keith said there was some resistance at first. The college had previously used the more standard model of diversity training, so he heard people question why they had to go through it *again*. "But they were pleasantly surprised because our new initiative wasn't just about diversity but a broad range of behaviors, and there were real-life applications throughout. It was very practical." (In fact, he added, the college did refresher courses not long ago, and he didn't hear a lot of concerns because people had seen the value from the first round of training.)

Providing training upfront to all college staff was valuable for two reasons: First, it provided people with the tools and language to talk about civil treatment issues. Second, it provided a forum where people could have conversations about sensitive issues. "It's very difficult to talk about behavioral issues in the course of a normal workday, and having a structured setting where people were face to face provided a forum where some of those issues could be raised," Keith said.

To make sure that the issues are kept in front of everyone, Keith added responsibility for ongoing diversity activities to an executive administrative position at the college. It is that person's job to oversee the implementation and make sure that diversity is interwoven into college operations. "One mistake some colleges and other organizations make is creating an office of diversity, because the rest of the organization begins to believe that diversity is *that office's* responsibility," said Keith. "I made diversity just one aspect of one executive's job, so the rest of us see that diversity is really *everyone's* responsibility."

There were many other elements to the initiative. "I didn't want civil treatment and diversity to be something that only got mentioned once a year," he added. "So we have a lot of discussions around diversity and civil treatment." The actions used to reinforce civil treatment needn't be elaborate, he added. For example, diversity is included as a topic on the agendas of many departmental meetings. "Even if they only talk about it for two minutes, it demonstrates that the department is keeping the topic alive and this isn't just an initiative that the president wants done," said Keith.

The college also took steps like adding diversity into regular performance evaluations. "That way, we knew that the topic would be raised at least every time a supervisor sat down with an employee," Keith explained.

Because the GTC initiative is still relatively new, the college has few measurable indicators of change. But Keith said his experiences are very different now. "Years ago, our culture wouldn't allow people to speak up if there were problems. Now, I see people speaking up more to bring something to our attention," he said. "If people see something happening that goes against how we said we wanted to treat each other, they will question it."

Keith believes that the concept of civil treatment and the concepts taught to college staff are well on their way to becoming embedded in the culture. "I think the changes we've made will stick around because people have seen the value in it," he said.

# CHAPTER 11

# Putting a Leadership Stake in the Ground

Along time ago, a colleague and I met with a client's senior compliance official. Like me, he was a lawyer by training though an executive by profession. He took us to a display case and showed us the awards his company's training programs had won for design excellence. No doubt they had great content and compelling exercises. He showed a parent's pride as he described their cutting-edge design.

Then the three of us went to a conference room and sat down to talk. He shut the doors and told us again how great his company's training programs were, then added that he had one major problem—he did not know how to get senior executives to personally take them (as opposed to having others sign in and take the courses at their request). When the organization's leaders can't be bothered to take civil treatment seriously, why should anyone else? That's not the way to build respect for values of any kind or translate principles into actions.

Years later, I met with the CEO of a big firm. He turned to his general counsel and said, "So ... do we have any employment cases going on?" I thought it was telling that he didn't already know. Even the behaviors at the top of the uncivil behavior pyramid—the overtly illegal behaviors—were barely on his radar. If the behaviors with the most obvious impact were only peripherally noticeable to the CEO, think about what that means for all the uncivil-but-technically-legal behaviors! If he wasn't paying attention to civil treatment, what are the odds that any other leader was?

Here's a third experience along the same lines: My firm worked with an academic institution where the HR group was very interested in changing behavior. We had trained various groups, but the deans and department heads were not included in the effort. That meant there was no voice from the top saying, "This is important." And while some improvements were made, the institution did not see the kinds of benefits that provided the impetus to sustain and expand a civil treatment effort.

One last example to kick off this chapter: Many years ago, I worked with a company that had all the right values written down. One day, I flew a thousand miles to meet with the CEO of a major division and his direct reports. The night before my presentation, he took me and a few others out for a very cordial dinner. The next day, just before the start of my presentation to his full team, he pulled me aside and said he'd forgotten to mention that he had scheduled a conference call for the same time and would not attend. He did not show up even to make opening remarks. His absence and the reason he couldn't attend was a powerful message to the other executives about how unimportant he regarded this subject.

The path of any successful, sustained major effort that led to beneficial culture change would look quite different from all those examples. The effort would have begun in earnest when senior leaders put a stake in the ground and said to the workforce, "This is what we need to do." It would have taken root when leaders walked their talk and demonstrated by their actions that the new direction was a priority. It would have begun to flourish as leaders repeatedly communicated their expectation that the effort would take time and that employee commitment and support was needed. It would have been sustained when employees realized there were positive consequences when they behaved in ways consistent with the new direction and negative consequences when they did not.

Once you've thought through the fundamental issues (as described in Chapter 10), your immediate focus should shift to creating the kind of leadership support required to make your initiative a success. There are many elements that go into an effective strategy and many challenges to overcome, but the bottom line is that your organization won't reach the destination of its civil treatment journey if you don't have leadership buy-in and commitment.

Sounds like a straightforward recipe for guaranteed success, doesn't it? But as we all know, making it happen in real life is never so simple. While leaders are, by and large, primed to take action when a disaster is staring them in the face, most seem unable to recognize the catastrophe-in-waiting represented by uncivil behaviors.

In this chapter, I talk about how to prepare your leaders for their role in preventing behavioral disasters and creating a more productive, inclusive, and diverse workplace culture. The issues for leaders fall generally into three categories:

A. Are your senior leaders aware of the issues and their impact? Meaning, do they see these behavioral issues as serious business problems affecting core business responsibilities?

B. Have you prepared them for their role?

C. Are they engaged in making civil treatment a reality?

## A. Educating Leaders About the Impact

You've just invested energy in creating a solid business case, right? (See Chapter 10.) Now is the time to use it to convince all key leaders, both inside and outside the enterprise (such as board members), that it is important to pay attention to civility. These are the people responsible for shaping the direction of the enterprise, looking at how it operates, and judging whether the initiative is in the organization's strategic interests. These influencers have to not just be convinced the principles are important, but be willing to actually apply and enforce them.

If you're lucky, your senior leaders will already understand the benefit of creating an organization guided by values-based actions. If they are not aware of the issues, don't see them as serious, or see these issues as being the sole responsibility of others lower in the organization's hierarchy—that is, as a *departmental* issue not a *business issue*—then you have a lot of work to do.

However, even if your senior leaders are not onboard initially, there are specific steps you can take to shift the tide in your favor. To reach a leader, you need to provide them with proof of impact, which is where the business case you will have developed (discussed in the previous chapter) comes in. Use the arguments you've assembled so that you can focus every conversation with an executive on how a civil treatment initiative links to their business objectives. Don't flood them with reports, studies, and legal cases drawn from other organizations—you need to get them to realize how different behaviors can impact *their* effectiveness personally and the organization's upon which they are judged.

Also, you can bring executives together and ask them to identify their biggest operational concerns. Likely they will identify retention, safety, quality, productivity, brand image, talent management, financial results, or other similar concerns. These are the issues they worry about and the ones that they must understand can be positively affected by civil behavior. Then show them how uncivil behavior (or violations of other standards) can seriously harm their operational concerns.

---

**Remember the benefit of simulations and case studies**

The educational importance of simulations and case studies was addressed back in Chapter 8. They are particularly useful when it comes to educating executives. My company, for example, uses short case studies that describe people exhibiting undesirable behaviors. We ask leaders to identify notable behaviors in the cases, positive or negative, and then identify the business detriments or benefits those behaviors cause. When done correctly, this kind of discussion helps leaders quickly realize how undesirable behaviors lead to harm but provide no business benefit—and that's the point.

---

# B. Preparing Leaders for Their Role

A good friend of mine was charged with building a global inclusion strategy for a world-renowned pharmaceutical firm. We've always had vigorous debates, and neither one of us backs down. He told me about advances his firm was making in learning. Because there are now multiple delivery platforms, his company's leaders can easily access learning modules on topics such as how to hire and engage new employees. There are avatars that can be adapted to simulate situations in different nations and cultures. My friend raved about the multiple apps for learning and completing just about every task.

I decided to challenge him about the role of canned training modules. I said, "If relying on one-size-fits-all packaged training and avatars and all that other stuff alone is so great ... tell me, what apps are you going to use to teach your grandson to be kind, ethical, decent, and honorable, just like you? Where are you going to find the app for that?"

He paused. Then he looked me dead in the eye and said, "I'm the app. That's my job. **I'm the app.**"

And that's the point. Some lessons, especially those dealing with how we act and apply values, have to be delivered by the right instructor outside of any formal classroom environment. The learning platform must be *human*—direct and credible. There's no technology, no inter-activity, no Learning Management System, and no clever avatar that can replace the power of a grandparent saying to a grandchild, "This is important. I want you to remember this. Here's a lesson you've got to learn to live and work by."

The same is true for instilling values and civil behaviors in the workplace. While classroom or online instruction has a role to play, there's no replacement for having leaders who are prepared to be living apps: a real-time aid to help people understand what's important and how their conduct is contributing to or preventing achievement of business goals. Sometimes, like my friend, we as leaders must say, "*Some lessons have to come from me, in real time, to be heard, understood, and applied. For those vital lessons, I'm the app.*"

What does it mean for a leader to be a living app? Their role is so critical that I've developed a model that I call CT Leader Actions for Leaders. This is a behavioral framework that helps leaders transform organizational initiatives into enduring cultural practices.

## 1) Model the behaviors and make sure employee behavior is consistent with civil values

We all know that what leaders say matters, but it's their behaviors that have a far bigger impact on employees. Employees mimic the actions and approaches of leaders, whether the examples are positive or, as we saw with the surgeon from Hospital X, negative. Therefore, it's the behavior of senior leaders that ultimately determines whether a major change is successful. How they act is seen as a measure of how to perform and what's acceptable. People learn to appreciate that behaviors linked to any value standards are important when leaders practice them daily. If leaders *don't* demonstrate that the messages they are imparting are important to their organization, people working with those leaders will ignore the messages, too.

---

### Real-life living apps

One example of a leader who is a living app is Jo Shapiro, Chief of Otolaryngology and Director of the Professionalism Center she helped establish at Harvard-affiliated Brigham and Women's Hospital (see Case 1). In addition to using checklists, she starts all of her surgeries by asking all in attendance to introduce themselves. She also reminds them of the important role that everyone on the team has in taking care of the patient, and encourages them to speak up if they suspect there is a problem. This is a regular practice that sets a standard of civility and encourages people to raise concerns if they have any doubts about what is happening in the OR.

There is a corporate CEO who is setting the same kind of example. He is known to gather his direct reports around and say, "Civil behaviors are how we need to run the business to get the best results." Leaders who practice civil treatment themselves generate all the benefits I've talked about, including increased trust, improved teamwork, better retention of employees, increased productivity, and stronger brand ambassadors.

---

## 2) Communicate civil treatment values and integrate them into daily practices

Even if messages are sincere, they'll often be either forgotten or ignored if delivered infrequently. When it comes to changing a culture, constancy and sincerity trump canned eloquence. Leaders need to reinforce messages through everyday conversations, emphasizing issues such as:

- The need for civility and all it entails is driven by business needs. "Compliance with the law" is not sufficient for optimizing performance (as described in Chapter 1).

- The effort will take a long-term commitment.

- The goal is to create a permanent change.

- Championing civil treatment values is a priority for them.

- Recent examples of commendable behavior

The key words in the above paragraph are "daily" and "everyday." Doing a formal communication once or twice a year will *not* help to drive cultural change. A leader has to talk about values informally and regularly. I do this at the operational team meetings in my own organization because I want my employees to realize that what we help companies do is not just about making money for our business but about driving important changes in the workplace. I discuss how we need to practice what we teach other firms, and whenever appropriate add in references linking civil treatment to something of value to our firm.

## 3) Encourage education and application

What typically happens when a company takes a check-the-box approach to learning is that a supervisor tells an employee something like: "Next week you have to take that course. I know you're busy, but just get through it. If you need to, minimize the screen so you can do other work. The two hours will go quickly." The employee completes the course, and upon returning, either nothing happens or the supervisor may say, "I told you you'd survive it. You're cool until next year."

I get the message this supervisor is sending, don't you? "This training is a waste of time."

What needs to happen instead is that your leaders should complete the training first. They can and should then say to an employee, "You have to go through this course because it's important to me and the company. I did it and learned a lot. After you're done, we'll talk about it." And the leader should follow through afterwards, asking the person what they thought of different points in the training, if there was anything they didn't understand, and so on.

## 4) Hold people accountable

When their people do an outstanding job, leaders need to openly appreciate, compliment, and reward those behaviors. Equally important, they must act—immediately and preferably informally—when they see others engaging in overt or "grey area" behaviors. A simple "Hey, you're close to getting out of line here" can stop behaviors from progressing to a more damaging level. If a leader doesn't react, the message they'll communicate is: "We'll talk about stuff, but all we're going to do is talk." (There's more about rewarding the standard and enforcing any breaches in Chapter 12.)

## 5) Build an open, welcoming culture

There's one lesson I learned many years ago when I interviewed a number of employees who worked in a troubled nuclear power plant. The people were all anonymous to me: I was never told their names and they did not wear ID badges. A lot of people at this plant were filing charges with the Nuclear Regulatory Commission or Department of Labor concerning safety hazards or indicating they were afraid to speak up about issues at the plant for fear of retaliation. This was not just an administrative nuisance for lawyers to sort out or settle. In the nuclear world, there was a fear that the government could use its regulatory powers to shut down troubled plants until any problems were sorted out and effective steps to change culture put into place. (When I held these interviews, it was estimated that such shutdowns would cost the facility more than a million dollars a day.)

I remember one person's comment in particular: "You have to have a manager who will listen *all the time* whenever issues arise, whatever they are. Otherwise you just won't talk to that person when you think there's a problem but aren't completely sure." The message was clear to me: in order for employees to trust that managers will react appropriately to *serious* issues, they and their manager need to have a history of dealing with *minor* issues.

As I talked about earlier, creating a culture that welcomes concerns is one of the most critical steps you can take towards achieving civil treatment. Getting employees to bring up concerns and report possible problems is difficult for a variety of reasons. That's why leaders have to continually encourage people to come forward with problems. They must listen carefully, non-judgmentally, and with appreciation, using the model described in Chapter 4. How small concerns and ideas are handled will determine how comfortable individuals feel about raising large, potentially serious matters. This includes the verbal and non-verbal behavioral markers that say "we mean it."

## 6) Deal with ambiguity

Recently, I met with a bright and talented CFO who had all the educational and workplace credentials you can imagine. I talked with him about the importance of guarding behavior in terms of abusive terms, sexual jokes—the usual litany. He threw up his hands and said, "I can't handle this! It is just too ambiguous and I can't apply it. I will just say nothing and avoid all jokes and avoid all humor. This is too vague."

I replied with something like this: "You're the CFO of a multi-billion-dollar company, right? I'm sure you are in the job because of your ability to deal with complexity and ambiguity, right? Are you saying that you can do your job effectively using judgment and analytical skills but not when it comes to dealing with people issues, which may also have complexity and ambiguity?" He didn't have an answer.

This CFO's attitude is unfortunate but not uncommon. Again and again I've been forced to realize how difficult it is for some business leaders, academics, and physicians to deal with grey areas—situations that are not expressly illegal and/or behaviorally ambiguous in isolation but, in their pattern, obviously toxic. The people I meet want clear examples and rules for every situation they might encounter. In essence, they are saying, "Yes, we know the blatant stuff. But we need to know how to definitively handle every grey area case."

Cut-and-dried rules may work in some circumstances, but odds are good that as a leader you will get involved in tough areas where

---

### When leaders need help

The corollary to item 6 is getting your leaders to seek help when situations are beyond their scope of experience. It's not an easy hurdle to overcome; many leaders think they should be able to handle behavioral issues on their own.

This is ironic because they *will* seek help in other circumstances. I've worked with excellent lawyers who don't hesitate to seek advice and input from colleagues to find solutions to ambiguous problems in their practice. But they balk if someone suggests they "seek advice and input" in cases involving a human resource issue outside their field of expertise. The same is true for many other leaders. Businesspeople will ask a colleague or direct report for an opinion about a strategic issue but don't want to ask for help when dealing with civility or behavioral problems. Physicians frequently seek advice and input from colleagues to find solutions to ambiguous problems in their medical practices but do not do the same with issues involving a human resource challenge. Academics are required to use rigorous testing and careful analysis of hypotheses, but many object to applying the same disciplines to complex people issues.

The key point is that competent leadership in ambiguous situations often involves getting help and recognizing that many people problems are complex—just like the professional and business challenges that outstanding leaders in any field encounter and address every day.

---

decisions are not clear. Leaders are most needed when behaviors are in the grey area and it's not clear whether those behaviors have crossed a line or violated a code of conduct, whether the behavior is merely a nettlesome business issue or something that requires careful factual analysis and an examination of the issues. That's when a leader's judgment and understanding of all of an organization's business interests are vital.

It is the ability to deal with the grey and ambiguous that provides a significant advantage for a "living app" leader. Leaders who are willing to accept and embrace their responsibility recognize that developing an ability to deal with grey areas makes them a formidable asset for a company.

## 7) Follow up and reinforce

Leaders who consistently apply their new set of skills and behaviors will help change the cultural standards of conduct in their organizations. Various forms of leader-driven reinforcement were described in Chapter 8.

## 8) Participate in learning

In the many, many behavioral initiatives I have witnessed over the years, it has been discouraging to see how many executives claim they are too busy to invest their time in learning about civil behaviors, and how many organizations buy that argument. According to a survey released in July 2015 by NAVEX Global, "senior leader training dropped by nearly 90 minutes ... in the past year."[14] That is a troubling trend since

---

14 http://blogs.wsj.com/riskandcompliance/2015/07/14/
the-morning-risk-report-compliance-training-time-drops-for-boards-executives/

we know that leadership modeling will be critical to embedding civil treatment in any organization.

Here's what I've learned: Leaders who avoid learning entirely—or demand very quick training—either don't really see these topics as personally important or they believe there isn't a messenger who will deliver a presentation worthy of their time. Their attitude is apparently *"All I want to do is get it over with—spend an hour a year, at most, doing the mandatory online course, then check the box. I need to spend my time making deals [conducting research, treating patients, planning, etc.]."* Leaders like these view civility, ethics, or other learning activities as a chore, unimportant in terms of their work—so the least time they need to spend, the least effort devoted, all the better.

I've often wondered why there's such an aversion to forcing senior leaders to participate in training sessions, let alone get involved in discussions and presentations on topics such as ethics, lawful behavior, and values that are very clearly tied to organizational health. This is also puzzling because errors at the top, whether violations committed by leaders or a failure to correct those of others, are frequently the most catastrophic.

If there is going to be equal enforcement of civility standards for leaders, they have to be prepared for their role in ways comparable to what you will provide to employees. Because their participation, support, and active sponsorship are so important, it's critical that learning experiences for this group be carefully designed and structured and professionally delivered. Simply sending them to training won't work.

Chapter 8 addressed how to create learning experiences that are rewarding for the audience, be it frontline or executive suite. The basic message there is that you need to make sure that all leaders at all levels get appropriate information and, equally importantly, the chance to practice their skills and think through what they are going to do differently on a daily basis.

Your senior leaders will be unprepared to fulfill their role as ambassadors of civil behavior if all they do is endorse a statement. They have to be prepared the same way as others in your organization through a mix of training, discussions, experience, and reinforcement so that they will understand how civility is being defined in your organization, what is required of them personally, and what procedures are being put in place to make sure old patterns of behavior are replaced.

## C. Getting Leaders Engaged in the Initiative

Through the years, I've seen some organizational leaders signal their commitment by requiring *others* to change. They will approve policies, statements, training, and communication initiatives but exempt themselves from the deployment process by finding "more important" things to do.

Not at Greenville Technical College, the case study that preceded this chapter. I was impressed by the way the college president, Keith Miller, modeled the change he wanted to see and truly became a role model. He had expressed to the leadership team his commitment to the initiative and explained why it was important to his direct reports. He charged them with attending an executive training session so they could both learn the college's new standards and also experience what other employees would go through. Each leader had to work out how they could model civility and bring it to their own teams.

Greenville Tech's small team of educators is starting the process by working on *themselves*. That's unusual and, in my judgment, vital. It establishes credibility and helps create a model that can spread effectively through the organization. These leaders were the first to take the training. They made the commitment to take personal and ongoing actions before trying to reach others in their organization. They pledged to communicate in their own words their commitment to inclusion, civility, and professionalism and to bring up behavioral values and issues during routine interactions with their teams. Each team member has developed a personal message, journals his or her interactions, and marks the impact the communications have on his/her team. In their own senior groups, they've started to discuss how this is affecting their teams.

Greenville's leaders have also agreed to speak up regularly. They've even developed some words of "course correction" when they want to point out a problem with what others in their group may have said, how they may have acted, and the impact their conduct may have had on individuals and the team. They are also keeping notes on how they do this and the impact it has on their interactions. Time will tell how enduring these actions prove, but the fact that they were initiated and that they have energized their team is a positive sign. Additionally, this group has been honest by acknowledging that they need to work on (a) their own communication skills, (b) including people who are different from themselves, and (c) listening to feedback regarding their own interactions.

In your own organization, you need to make sure that leaders are given responsibilities that they can act upon regularly so they can continually be engaged. Even if you don't take it as far as Greenville has gone, make sure they are visibly leading the effort. Having them play an active role serves several functions:

1) It shows that the message is not just a top-level communication but that leaders at all levels have roles in delivering and maintaining it.

2) When top-level leaders have to communicate with, explain, and in that sense teach others, they also have to learn—and the process of having to periodically talk about key themes helps refresh and embed their own learning.

3) Ideally, your prepared leaders will become teachers in turn. When they talk about, demonstrate, and reinforce key learning messages, they help remind their teams, and themselves, about what's important, why it's important, and how to act in line with key learning themes. That's how key lessons change behavior and are transmitted from one workplace generation to the next. When they communicate or teach small lessons, their teams hear the messages more than one time annually and it reinforces what they must learn and absorb as well.

# Summary: The Commitment Lodestar

Efforts linked to values and behavior can't be labeled as a human resource initiative or a risk management process, can't be driven solely by legal counsel or compliance officers; they must be initiated and directed by senior leaders responsible for the overall direction of the enterprise. Without active, personally engaged executive leadership, civility won't be taken seriously and won't take root because it won't be seen as having a business purpose. Your leaders need to actively support it, communicate their expectations that all employees do the same, and demonstrate with their own behavior that it's important to them personally. If any piece of this pattern is missing, employees will immediately pick up on the mismatch and perceive that the change isn't that important after all.

I like to point out to organizations that getting leaders involved in launching and supporting civil treatment efforts is one of the cheapest ways to see real change. For a little bit of executive time, they will see a huge uptick in employee engagement. In fact, you can tell if an organization is really committed to a culture change initiative by looking at whether senior leaders are actively engaged in the initiative or just giving it token support. There's no great wisdom in this observation.

As it's long been said, and rightly so, "talk is cheap" and often in plentiful supply. Now, don't get me wrong. Effective leaders will talk about their commitment to values all the time, not once a year or in press interviews and annual shareholder meetings. But they will follow up that talk with actions that demonstrate they mean what they say, and they will work to bring others up to the same standards. By their actions they will make clear to others that what we are calling civil treatment is driven by business realities and is not simply a passing fad or one-time training initiative.

# CHAPTER 12

# Planning for Launch and Beyond

**D**esigning a future workplace is often approached as a philosophical and aspirational exercise rather than the development of a practical plan to accomplish concrete business and organizational objectives. The question that needs to be asked is how you should approach this cultural initiative to make sure that you get behavioral results you can identify, measure, and track—as opposed to simply creating a general vision and mood.

As a child of the '60s, to me the term "successful launch" always conjures up an image of a spacecraft being shot into orbit. While trying to change a culture is a different mission than blasting off from Cape Canaveral, that term has a similar meaning: In both cases, a successful launch is not simply based on executing the start of the event. It must take into account much more.

When the Mercury spacecraft was about to lift off with astronaut John Glenn in the cockpit, NASA's work did not end with figuring out how to get the space capsule to circle the Earth. Those who meticulously planned the event didn't say, "Let's do everything to get John Glenn in space and then see what happens!" That key moment was a critical step, but only the start of the journey. NASA's engineers needed to contemplate a range of steps from ignition, to liftoff, reaching the apogee of the flight, preparing for reentry, and finally touchdown. They wanted to be ready for any contingency and to counter any risks that could derail the flight and lead to catastrophe. What if there was an engine failure, or radio communications broke down, or some other unwanted event caused the flight plan to change? What if the space-craft ended up landing far away from where the recovery vessels waited at sea? The whole mission could fail if one of those steps did.

In contrast to NASA's model, organizational initiatives are often launched without considering all the pieces that must be in place and all that could happen once the first phase is started. That oversight sows the seeds for failure even before the initiative starts. As with a successful orbital flight, knowing a mission's objective and starting is, of course, critical, but it's just not enough to maximize the odds for success.

While we can't prepare for every possible contingency in the launch of a civil treatment initiative, there are several major areas to address and problems to anticipate that can increase the chance for long-term success. If you've done the foundational work described in the previous chapter, you should know what it is your organization wants to accomplish. You've prepared your top leaders, and now it's time to branch out the deployment, which should include:

1) Engaging local line managers to lead the effort and to keep actively engaged as a sign of commitment.

2) Preparing employees.

3) Establishing consequences for civil and uncivil behavior (rewarding the standard; enforce the breach).

4) Identifying indicators of success.

5) Developing plans to sustain learning and key behavioral changes.

# 1) Engaging Line Leaders Sooner, Not Later

Many organizations launch civility initiatives from the top and don't involve local leaders in the planning or the execution. As discussed in a previous chapter, getting senior leader buy-in and involvement is critical, but they are not the only critical players: much of the success of a rollout will depend on how well your line leaders bring civil treatment to life.

Since local leaders will ultimately become the guardians of the process in the day-to-day actions in the portion of your company that they control, it is shortsighted to exempt them in planning how the initiative will look in your organization. They need to demonstrate through what they do that the initiative is really part of everyone's day-to-day responsibilities. And they're the ones who will have to address and head off resistance and outright opposition, purposeful or habitual, whenever it arises.

I learned this lesson years ago on my first real job as a part-time salesperson for a company called Baker's Shoes. Back in those days, there wasn't any such thing as employee orientation, and no training. I may have gotten some basic rules to review, but what really stuck out was what my boss told me and lived up to on my job. In fact, that's what I remember now nearly 50 years later.

Right before my first day of work, my boss, Joseph Silverman, told me how much I would be paid, what I would do, and my shift hours. Finally, he said, "Baker's takes pride in showing respect for our customers. So be here at 8:30 a.m. Saturday. Wear a white shirt and a dark suit."

There was one problem: I had only one heavy grey wool suit, which had been given to me by a friend for a role in the prior year's class play. If I wore that suit, I knew I would burn up, sweat, and itch on that sweltering day in an un-air-conditioned shoe store. I could imagine the wool itching against my skin and knew I wouldn't be able to walk a step without feeling uncomfortable. (This was my "conceptual resistance" to wearing a dark suit.)

So I wore my solid lightweight dark-blue blazer with matching blue slacks. The blazer buttons were gold, but to my eye it looked just like a suit, and I would be more comfortable. I arrived at work on time, greeted by Mr. Silverman, who wore a dark suit and white shirt. His first reaction just as I entered the store: "Where's the suit?"

"But it's hot and this is just like a suit," I replied.

Mr. Silverman said, "I said a suit, not *just like* a suit. Go home and come back in a suit if you have one. Otherwise, forget it. We all wear shirts and suits—that's how we do business here."

I went home and told my dad. Without hesitation, he ordered, "Put on your suit and get down there now." And so I did. I sweated that first day and first month until I could save enough to buy a real, lighter-weight suit.

Baker's did not spend a lot to get this message out. But because of the consistent enforcement by my direct supervisor—coupled with consequences for the failure to follow the rules—the company's dress code had become embedded in its culture. Mr. Silverman always wore a suit and white shirt, he communicated this rule for behavior to every employee before they started, and he enforced it. It was clear, important and he brooked no exceptions. (Years later, in my professional life, it took me a long time to add solid blue to my collection of otherwise solid white business shirts.)

My Baker's Shoes experience taught me many lessons. One was the importance of having simple messages that are linked to specific behaviors. "Wear a white shirt and a dark suit" isn't so very different from "don't scream at and don't direct racial, sexual, or other like comments to co-workers and customers." Another lesson that has risen in importance over the years for me: the critical role that local leaders have in building culture. As I've said before, without the daily actions of middle and frontline management, true cultural change in any organization is not going to happen.

Too many companies focus only on the executive levels or only on frontline staff and miss this very powerful driver of change represented by middle management and informal leaders. These local leaders have responsibilities similar to those of the senior leaders. They may not make the decision as to how civility will be applied, but they have to follow and support the new standard. This means:

- They must sincerely support the top leaders' commitments.

- They cannot just mouth the words; their behavior must match.

- They must be the continuing education of the initiative—be another type of "living app" just like senior leaders.

- They must be willing to hold everyone (including top performers) accountable.

You need to make your expectations clear around all of their business responsibilities—legal and civil—and continually plan to reinforce the expectation that leaders will step in immediately if they see deviations from your standards.

## 2) Educate and Prepare Employees

Throughout the book, I've talked a lot about the importance of having leadership active, involved, and prepared for their role. However, civil treatment needs to touch every employee throughout an organization if it is to become a cultural standard and lead to the benefits previously discussed. The vast majority of internal interactions are employee to employee, and the vast majority of interactions between your organization and the outside world are through your employees. Those interactions are very powerful, for better or for worse, and have a viral spread. If a key employee shows a lack of enthusiasm about civil treatment or lack of commitment to your organizational vision, or has problems that appear somewhere along the spectrum of the bad behaviors outlined in Chapter 2, you can bet their attitudes and behaviors will spread to others. That can have a serious impact on the climate and long-term culture of the organization. Fortunately, the flipside is true as well: if key employees demonstrate civil treatment, their behavior can establish new norms for your organization.

In short, performance within groups *irrespective of whether it involves a leader* will affect organizational performance positively or negatively. So when it comes to implementation, you can't gloss over the involvement, engagement, and education of employees. Unfortunately, too many organizations put too little effort into involving employees in the civil treatment changes, perhaps because of:

- **The skewed perception of lower risk.** All managers are charged with acting legally for their company, hence the perception that it's managers' behavior that poses the greatest risk. That may be true in terms of legal risk—that is, the top of the uncivil triangle where management liability arises—but it is not true for all of the "legal but uncivil behaviors" that form the bulk of the uncivil triangle. Employees can be just as prone to toxic behaviors as leaders, and *that* poses risks above and beyond legal consequence.

- **A focus on short-term dollar costs associated with lost productivity** (versus the potential long-term gains in productivity from a more civil workplace). Organizations that focus almost solely on the costs of instruction (including the time employees must spend away from their jobs) may believe they can't afford to give people instruction on civility and ethics, and decide to do the absolute minimum needed to establish a defense claim ("It was the employee's fault for doing the wrong thing—after all, they were trained!"). They are overlooking the ongoing business gains they can make that will more than repay the costs of the initial investment.

Don't make the mistake of buying into these false assumptions. When employees demonstrate improper behaviors among themselves or fail to alert the organization to problems and hazards, it causes harm and spreads to others. That's why, when it comes time for implementation, you have to give adequate attention to your workforce. For a civil treatment initiative to take root, they must be involved, must accept key premises, and must have ongoing responsibilities clearly defined in terms of their behavior and how to raise issues if they feel key principles are not being followed.

As discussed in Part II, the purpose here is not just to communicate information but to persuade people to adopt and sustain new skills and behaviors. If all you do is tell the organization that you want everyone to be civil, guess what will happen? Nothing. That's why messages from the organization and from direct leaders must be carefully planned and coordinated. Workplace learning and skills practice (e.g., training) must be structured so that the significance of civility efforts is clearly understood.

# 3) Reward the Standard; Enforce the Breach

For your cultural changes to matter, there must be consequences: recognition for those who meet standards and consequences for those whose conduct fails to meet the expected standard. Without consequences, new standards simply won't matter to your workforce.

When it comes to reinforcing and recognizing people who embody your values and civil treatment, I'd point you to the many, many other kinds of reward programs that companies have. I've seen many such awards presented to people who achieve particular sales goals or those who demonstrate a strong commitment to safety, for example. Since civil treatment is important to obtaining business results, why not do the same thing for people who demonstrate key civil behaviors linked to business results?

The idea is that this kind of recognition also helps to foster desired behaviors going forward. A few years ago, for example, my company established an award named in honor of George H. Kaye, who was the VP of human resources at Brigham and Women's Hospital for many years. He was also one of my mentors and a man I admired greatly. Our George H. Kaye award is therefore given to someone who epitomizes our values (cooperation, inclusion, teamwork, integrity). The first employee to win the award certainly met all those criteria. A year later, I overheard another employee comment that the winner had been pushing really hard on a particular project. And the winner replied, "I won the Kaye award." A year later and the recognition she received was still providing an incentive for high performance.

## Enforcing the breach

When employees fail to live up to your standards, you also have to take action. The first question you face is whether the breach requires action. Here's a checklist that I use to help leaders sort through that question:

- Does the behavior consist of comments, jokes, or remarks that have racial, sexual, religious, or other content that demeans a particular group of persons? Quite often such grey-area conduct is seen as innocent because it does not have explicitly taboo words or images. A single event may be a one-time lapse in judgment. But it's probably not an accident or harmless if it forms an ongoing pattern.

- Does the conduct involve actions, such as excluding others from social groups, failing to recognize them in meetings or discussions, or dismissive body language or tone of voice?

- Does the behavior affect a single individual or several people?

- Have multiple people commented or complained to leadership about such conduct?

- Has the person engaging in the behavior been warned or counseled or even spoken to at any time about the behavior?

- Has the individual repeated the behavior even after being told it is unacceptable?

The more frequently the above signs appear, the more likely it is that there's a problem that leaders need to address. If your reaction when hearing about a breach is something like, "Well, that's just the way he or she is. They don't mean anything by it." —that indicates a pattern of behavior, not a momentary lapse in judgment. The issues will likely get worse and continue escalating in impact until you take action to stop it.

When you determine that breaches have occurred, you should have a behavioral model for responding that is consistent for all leaders in your organization. I described one model in Chapter 4, but your organization may already have one of its own. Either way, the key is that every leader in the organization needs to know when and how to use it.

## *Equal enforcement for Big Shots*

Getting any of us to change ingrained habits is extremely challenging. And the hurdle is often bigger for one sector of employees: the Big Shots—prominent leaders or big contributors who have always received special treatment and been able to do whatever they've wanted. It's best to anticipate that some Big Shots will have enormous conceptual resistance to adopting new behaviors. Unless the Big Shot's uncivil behavior is extraordinarily improper, verging on the most flagrant violations or expressly illegal acts, many leaders will be inclined to look the other way so as not to lose top performers and the value they bring. The chapters in Part I, however, made it clear that if such conduct is ignored, the cost is a loss of leadership credibility: people will stop believing that civil behavior matters, that it is tied to business needs, and that it applies to everyone.

Leaders or Big Shots of any sort often think they are subject to *special rules* (it's part of their conceptual resistance). And they're right—but not in the way they think. In today's world, emails, voicemails, pictures, and videos capturing proof of poor or inappropriate behavior can get circulated around the planet instantly. The rules for leaders *are* special because new technologies allow the acceleration of their fall to reach warp speed in breathtaking quickness, leading not only to career damage but also to personal harm and their worst nightmare, lasting humiliation. And their misdeeds and misbehavior can damage the brands of their organizations due to their prominence.

As a special part of your launch planning, both to avoid problems and demonstrate a commitment to making real changes, it's important to have a strategy for preventing Big Shot misbehavior and addressing it thoughtfully when it arises. How their cases are handled will have a profound impact on the organization and the initiative itself. That means helping them replace bad habits with good ones. They need to understand how to address—in terms of what to say, the tone and body language—their issues and that it is best to deliver criticism to others in quiet, private areas. If the Big Shot's behavior does cross normal boundaries, they also need to understand this and know how to apologize.

Once the destructive performers begin to recognize their behavior is counter to the very goals for which they strive, hopefully, they'll begin to practice new habits that will lead them and their respective organizations to positive outcomes. If they don't, leaders will face a stark choice: either tolerate disruptive performers, accepting the harm their behaviors engender, or remove offenders to safeguard not only the organization's values, but also their own business responsibilities.

I've written several times in this book about the unwillingness of Hospital X, which employed the "surgeons gone wild," to take action. An example from a different hospital shows how these disruptive surgeons should have been handled. It's a model any organization can adapt and apply to its own circumstances.

When serving as the head of a department, an internationally renowned physician was consistent in communicating his expectations about behavior to all his team, but there was one physician who did not change. Finally, this department head met with the uncooperative physician one on one and said, "This is coming from me. You are either going to change your behavior or you won't be working here much longer." After that conversation, the institution took the following steps (since we know that one-time experiences are rarely enough to change ingrained behavior):

- **Provided clear behavioral guidelines and expectations for the Big Shot's behavior.** As amazing as it sounds, I have met a number of people who don't know that screaming, yelling, shouting down dissent, and even humiliating others are unacceptable!

- **Helped the physician understand the impact of his behavior on others**. He needed to see the potential impact his behavior could have on the people who served his patients (and potentially directly on the patients as well).

- **Gave him a chance to practice new behaviors in a safe setting**. This hospital set up simulations that re-created situations where the physician had acted improperly in the past. Running through the simulation with a new strategy in mind got the physician to see how it felt to apply a new behavioral model.

- **Provided judicious coaching and feedback on the person's progress**. You don't want to hover over a Big Shot's shoulder—that wouldn't work well for anyone!—but you can't expect them to be perfect right out of the gate either. This institution checked in occasionally with the physician and asked him to describe situations he'd faced recently and how he'd dealt with them.

- **Told him how and how often his conduct would be formally evaluated**. This hospital advised the physician his conduct would be evaluated at distinct intervals by a departmental committee and followed through on that commitment.

Beyond these steps, the organization's leaders also communicated this plan of action to other employees—that is, they made it clear that the consequences for poor behavior were the same for *all* employees.

While the specifics will vary depending on the type of misbehavior exhibited by a Big Shot, the model above is a good starting point. The Big Shot gets help understanding why what they did was wrong and knows specifically what they are expected to change.

I'll end this section with a story about an explosive CEO who had started a successful, nationally known enterprise—but his explosive temper and outrageous behavior threatened to bring his firm the kind of publicity that would have quickly ruined him and it. I sat down with him and talked about the law. Yes, he agreed, the laws do apply to him. Then we spent most of our time discussing his own vulnerability, using stories I had found about other disgraced leaders on the internet. Neither he nor I could distinguish how his actions differed from those of the fallen leaders whose stories were so widely publicized. That got his attention.

I gave him an index-card-sized reminder with just a few suggestions, including obvious rules around what not to do or say and the meaning of professional conduct. But as you well know, it's not his understanding of the law that will change his behavior. The acid test will be whether he recognizes just how quickly the über-gravity of social media could bring him, as it has others, to the ground.

# 4) Evaluating Success

Many organizations don't develop a set of indicators *before* they launch an initiative and therefore have to scramble to develop measurements after the process has already begun. It's better to know ahead of time what you want to see in terms of progress and success so you'll know what to monitor and measure.

Thinking at the outset about how you're going to measure success forces you to ask yourself what's really important to your organization: *What do we want to achieve?* and *What is the value of what I am doing?* That will help focus on the metrics that would be useful for your organization specifically (as opposed to another organization).

It's likely your organization has completed prior initiatives that involved employee education, but it's likely that the learning goals here are different so the old measures of success might not apply. For example, if all you needed to do was make sure that information was disseminated to 100% of employees (perhaps for building a legal defense), then you would have measured success by documenting whether people received and signed off on documentation or completed a training module. Or perhaps a training department wanted to make sure that people enjoyed a training course and thought the content was relevant to their job, so their measures of success may have been knowing whether, say, 90% of employees enjoyed the educational experience and said they will use what they learned.

Obviously, no culture changes overnight, but there are steps you can take to evaluate whether you are headed down the right path. For each organization it will be different, just as the details of its culture will be, but here are some indicators to consider and measure.

Evaluating the gains from a change in culture is seldom easy because many improvements are intangible or indirect and they take time to accumulate. At times it seems that everyone will have a different definition of success. Yet while there is no real finish line, there are many ways to evaluate progress:

**1) Business results**

- How are your products/services doing against different consumer demographics now versus before?

- Have you effectively used diversity to grow incremental dollars?

**2) Employment issues**

- How are you doing with retention and movement of people inside the organization?

- Is there reasonable parity internally in terms of promotions and externally in terms of hiring?

- What do employee insights surveys tell you about the policies and practices that affect employees?

### 3) Risk management

- Is the number of complaints or charges (of discrimination, for example) dropping?

- Are you effectively managing and resolving employee relations issues as they are raised?

- Are you facing additional litigation?

In general, think about what you would and would *not* see and experience if the effort were succeeding, and what you would or wouldn't see if it wasn't. What are the behavioral markers of success or failure? At the broadest level, you can evaluate success by answering this question: "Is our organization addressing ethics and civility with anything like the sort of emphasis on other important issues that affect performance and cause harm?"

Other indicators you can use to help you *predict* the potential for success based on whether you can answer "yes" to the following conditions:

- Leaders are convinced that a long-term investment is a business necessity.

- Leaders make culture change a priority for themselves rather than delegating the task to someone else to handle.

- Your organization has defined clear behaviors that define cultural standards.

- You know how to help leaders at all levels integrate desired standards into ongoing workplace conversations, education, and rewards.

- You are ready to enforce consequences for violations—even if, or rather particularly if, senior leaders or visible organizational stars commit them.

- You have built a plan supported by resources to obtain specific and measurable results, the same way you would with any other strategic business objective.

The items in the checklist, however, are process metrics for the deployment—they tell you if you have the right ingredients in place but don't reflect whether your organization is seeing the benefits of your initiative. Naturally, organizations also want to have some measures that help them evaluate implementation (how far and how fast and how well the civil treatment initiative is penetrating the organization) and outcomes, including what benefits the initiative has generated. Implementing a civility initiative is no different.

Some organizations will look at the before and after results of engagement surveys; others will take a look at whether internal complaints rise or fall; others will try to get an assessment of the immediate impact of learning, which is a useful but short-term measure; and others will periodically do spot-check anecdotal interviews with team members to get a sense of how things have changed in specific work

---

### Tracking leaders' progress

You may have noticed that a lot of the items in the checklist deal with leadership. As a way to help, make sure that they are on board and making process; get them (and others) to track how they apply key learnings on a daily basis. Make this task easy, perhaps by suggesting they spend as little as two to three minutes a day journaling their activities and impressions. When learners have to record what they are doing with regularity, it makes it more likely they'll continue to apply the same standards going forward.

Also, establish a process through which leaders report their activities. If leaders are not held accountable for doing this, it often won't get done. And when done well, it should lead to some form of positive recognition; when not done, just the opposite.

---

units. There are other metrics that may measure errors, productivity, and the like that are controlled for changes that link to civility initiatives.

Even more important than any specific indicator is the atmosphere that will permeate your organization if your civil treatment effort is successful. You'll see it and feel it around you every day. In my own organization, I take pride in seeing people make magnificent decisions on behalf of our clients and each other because they understand our values. They respond to clients and handle logistical, learning, and technical issues quickly and responsively. They do this on their own, and they know when to ask others for assistance. It's exciting and rewarding to see that happen. Clients get the best treatment, and we make the best decisions. It makes for a stronger, nimbler organization. The process is never done, however, and problems will arise. How we address them, whatever they involve, is part of our demonstrating that values really have meaning.

---

### Sources of information

You can measure success with quantitative and qualitative metrics gained through mechanisms such as:

- 360 surveys

- Engagement studies

- Changes in internal issues raised, retention, etc.

- Anecdotal interviews in different organizational areas

---

# 5) Planning to Sustain the Learning and Changes

This is the "what happens after the launch" step. That is, once you've gotten an astronaut into space, how do you keep him or her there? To address this question, I'd direct you to topics I've covered elsewhere in the book, such as:

- Chapter 8, which discussed how and when to use just-in-time refresher modules and combining multiple forms of reinforcement.

- The theme of Chapter 4, which was to be consistent in the use of new behavioral models.

- An earlier section of this chapter, which discussed enforcing consequences for both civil and uncivil behaviors.

Here's a new idea, too: ever thought of using internal marketing to help you sustain changes? Many organizations I have worked with have extraordinary marketing departments. But ironically they often do not use that capability in terms of "selling" the idea of civil treatment internally to their own employees. Marketing departments have people who are experts in getting other people to pay attention to and buy into certain ideas. Why not use that capability to help build support for civil treatment in your organization?

Have your marketing department help you craft concise customer-focused messages; engage them in developing communications that explain in brief terms why civil treatment matters in terms of daily business and that can serve to keep such messages alive and vibrant.

## Summary: Focus on Your Aims and Goals

This may sound like odd advice since I've talked about the complexities of dealing with behavioral issues and all of the details that have to come together to have a successful implementation, but if you feel your organization is getting overwhelmed, remember this: **simplicity is the name of the game**.

As you shape your own launch, then, focus on simple statements of what you want to achieve. What are the few priority messages you want to convey during a launch? What are the simplest and most effective ways to get those messages across? What simple, daily changes can you make to ensure that the changes take root?

Simple values and behaviors, consistently reinforced, are the most effective strategy for initiating, creating, and sustaining a culture that minimizes uncivil and illegal behaviors and deals quickly and effectively with such behaviors when they do appear.

*A former CEO of a nationally known medical organization** commented that teamwork "is about the complexity of relationships, problem solving, and working together toward a common goal." That focus on relationships gave rise to a mandatory professionalism program for physicians. My friend Catherine was a driving force in making that program a reality. Here's her story of how that happened.*

# Good Work Takes Good Teamwork

Twenty years ago, Catherine told me, one of the medical regulatory boards had just come out with the "six competencies" for physicians, one of which was professionalism.

"Because of the leadership of our then-CEO, my organization had decided to begin a leadership program for our physicians," said Catherine. (She notes that the word "professionalism" hadn't gained widespread acceptance at that time. Physicians talked more about "mutual respect." Today, the term "culture of safety" is often used.)

"This CEO was a builder of people and tough leader who understood that in order to do quality work, it took teamwork. He knew that leaders needed to meet their troops and foster respectful communication," Catherine said. At the time, she was chair of the institution's human resources committee and also the dean of an allied healthcare organization. It became her responsibility to develop what the organization labeled a "mutual respect" initiative.

---

\* The identity of this organization and the speaker have been disguised as their request.

The result was their leadership program, one of the first that became a mandatory course for all staff physicians. "We have formal programs and do case presentations to demonstrate that it's not only what people say but *how* they say it that's important," she said. "We use examples to demonstrate what good listening is and what leaders should and shouldn't say."

Catherine recalled a particular example from the early training that has continued resonating with audiences: a graphic showing that what gets people into trouble is "in the eye of the beholder" (using a phrase from the training). "So whether or not there was an offense couldn't be based on what I or my colleagues thought, but that third person in the room who overheard something or was offended by it," she said. "Twenty years later, we still talk about that concept frequently."

Naturally, they encountered a lot of questions and resistance at first. "Department heads questioned our ability to take physicians out of the workplace to provide the training and make sure it happened, so we had to deal with those issues. Sometimes, a physician said 'no.' What happened then was that either the CEO, who was also a physician, or I would have a one-on-one conversation with that person." As a result of that personal attention from senior leadership, the organization has had more than 99.9% participation in the leadership program over the past two decades.

Catherine says the program has made a huge difference in how people interact on a daily basis, and has helped the institution maintain its professional and even collegial atmosphere. "A lot of this is about fairness and listening," she commented. "We want our leaders to always make sure they are hearing at least two sides to every story." As a result, "the teamwork in my department has stayed strong for over 20 years," she noted.

# CHAPTER 13

# Creating Cultural Consistency

## *Across the Street or Around the Globe*

The U.S. CEO of a multi-billion-dollar global operation had recently led the acquisition of a smaller, highly profitable, closely held firm that had a long history of financial success. But the organizations could not work together. Naturally they had different processes; but in truth, those can be fixed. The real problem was that although on paper the two entities had the same values, in practice—meaning as expressed on a daily basis through behaviors in the workplace and how people interacted—they were in fact quite different. The CEO told me the acquired operation quickly went from profitable to unprofitable. He attributed this to a clash in cultures and the differences in how the acquiring and acquired entities not only did business internally but treated one another.

Between the growing frequency of mergers and acquisitions (M&A) and corporate globalism, it seems there are few companies these days that *don't* eventually have to deal with blending cultures. Leaders involved in global businesses or that get involved in M&A have an extraordinary challenge: how to create a consistent culture built around the organization's values despite having divisions or departments or branches that have very different histories or settings. The challenge can seem overwhelming because the differences in the environments where the business operates or in the accepted norms can be vast. Every aspect of human interaction is affected, from the types of jokes told to the manner of dress and body language. What is acceptable professionally and personally in one country or even one company is often seen as offensive or even discriminatory in another.

In this chapter, I want to explore the two main kinds of culture clash that organizations encounter: across societies and across different business environments. There are some differences but also a lot of similarity in how you would approach these two situations. The key is to find a way to be consistent within your organization but respectful of individual and societal differences.

## Dealing with Societal Differences

The most obvious clashes of culture occur when a business has offices or other facilities in various parts of the world. The key to dealing with these societal differences is to focus on what should be common to the organization, not what is different between the societies.

And there is a lot of commonality if you look closely, including basic civilities that apply universally. I don't know anyone anywhere who *wants* to be kidded or demeaned or passed over for promotion based on their national origin, religion, gender, race, age, color, or sexual orientation. I don't know anyone who wants to be paid unfairly. Similarly, when you ask people how they want to be treated in the workplace, you hear the same answers from people everywhere: They want to be respected and not mocked or demeaned because of their ethnicity, race, or other like characteristics. Everyone wants to feel safe. Everyone wants to feel they can contribute to their fullest and be recognized for their contributions.

Incorporating statements about universal issues like these could form the foundation of the values that an organization decides to embrace across all its locations, whether dozens or thousands of miles apart. Here are four other steps you can take to build a unified business culture.

## 1. Separate business culture from societal culture

The solution to the challenge of dealing with business commonalities and societal differences is demonstrated by a global firm we worked with years ago. The company held annual meetings in Europe that brought together people from many countries including Israel, Egypt, and others in the Middle East—countries that do not normally cooperate. When asked how they made sure their meetings were productive, the leaders of this company said, "We all have a common interest in making sure that our products sell well in every country. So we just talk about business."

Time and again, companies approach us who are struggling with how to think about their business environments because they know they can't alter the cultures in which their employees live. If you want to make inroads, you have to acknowledge that different cultures exist outside your workplace, then work to define what it takes to be successful in your organization and make sure all employees understand those standards.

Obviously, many companies today have to deal with global cultural issues all the time. The most effective approaches I've seen are based on the idea that the organization needs to establish common expectations for how people would be treated while at work, despite any differences in the cultures where the company's offices are located.

For example , in the U.S., behaviors that constitute sexual harassment are illegal. In some other cultures, such behaviors are not only legal but the norm. But allowing women to work in a safe environment is often a company value that needs to be enforced worldwide, so leadership must continually reinforce the message that their organization will not tolerate sexual harassment anywhere, whether or not it is technically legal in a particular location.

A business cannot and should not try to change the national cultures in which it operates. But the organization has a responsibility to create an organizational environment that makes it possible for work to get done most effectively and for all employees to be comfortable. Just as they would globally enforce best practices for any production or transaction processes that are critical to doing business and making a profit, they should enforce best practices for behavior. All employees must be treated as "citizens of the organization" wherever they live and work. This prevents the idea that civil treatment is a solely U.S.-centric initiative.

Above all, your leaders must be clear and forceful in spreading the message that your organization is not trying to change any society's culture, but they are setting standards for how everyone should work together inside the business. They must communicate that *to be successful in your organization* all employees are expected to follow the company's values, and that *within the business*, certain behaviors are acceptable or not acceptable because of the impact they have on the organization's ability to get work done. You will never be able to create a unified global business culture if your top leaders are not actively engaged in making it happen.

## 2. Make it simple

As I have written earlier, when employees are aware of the values that are important to their company and the purpose of those values, they don't need thousands of rules to guide their behavior. This is particularly critical in trying to create common global workplace cultures. Employees need a concrete framework that is easy to understand, easy to follow, and easy to enforce.

Think about the value of "respect," for example. There are hundreds of different ways in which people demonstrate respect for each other around the world. You can't hope to capture all the nuances in a massive document—that would be not only impractical but impossible. Instead, focus on some simple guidelines that explain why the business considers it important to be respectful in all situations and provide some simple examples (such as "everyone gets a chance to speak in meetings").

In fact, nowhere will simplicity have a bigger payback than when you are trying to make a cross-cultural approach workable. You must define a manageable set of values and provide examples of appropriate as well as unacceptable behaviors, then help communicate those values in a way that ensures *all* employees understand what the values mean in terms of workplace behavior. For example, offer learning opportunities so people can understand why the values and behaviors are important. Develop mechanisms where people can get clarification about what your organization expects.

## 3. Involve local leadership

The involvement of line leaders is particularly important for global organizations. Years ago, I worked with a pharmaceutical firm that wanted to launch a global civil treatment initiative. We suggested that they involve leaders from around the globe, but they chose to develop it internally from corporate. As soon as the other constituents were brought in, they objected, claiming the program was "corporate-centric" and "U.S.-centric" even though everything indicated it had not been designed that way. But the other parties felt excluded from the process, which is a key tenet of civil treatment, and they rejected the initiative.

Later, we engaged in a similar initiative with another major pharmaceutical firm and a nationally known consumer products firm, both of which involved local leaders to a greater extent than the pharmaceutical company. They both used essentially the same structural content we had proposed for the first organization but, in both instances, the focus on local involvement made a striking difference in the success and even the launch of the process.

## 4. Adapt to local environments as much as you can

My friend Phil Weis, who talked about learning strategies in a previous chapter, often gets involved in global deployments of initiatives. He told me about one company that was rolling out an internal hotline to handle employee complaints. The company had developed a training course explaining why it was important for employees to report non-compliance so the situation could be investigated and fixed if need be.

"We discovered that in some parts of the world, asking people to report their bosses would conflict with very strongly held values of respect and shame," he said. "In those cultures, reporting any known or suspected infractions would be equivalent to bringing shame on their bosses, which is something they would never, ever do."

The managers in those countries told Phil and his colleagues that if they simply tried to deploy the existing training program, which focused on reporting complaints, no one would listen to them.

"But the company really wanted to have employees bring issues to management's attention," said Phil. "So they had to think about how to achieve that goal in a different way in some places." The old environmental mantra of "think globally, act locally" applies to cultural change as well!

By engaging in discussion with local leaders, the company discovered that there was one value even more powerful than shame in these cultures, and that was integrity. "If someone was caught between acting with integrity and the potential of causing shame to a boss, they would go with integrity every time," explained Phil.

So the company adapted the implementation. They couldn't compel people to use a hotline to report concerns because that would bring shame on their manager or department. Instead, they started doing face-to-face interviews where they would ask an employee, "Have you encountered anything of concern that conflicts with our company policies?" In response to that direct question, people's integrity would more often than not overcome their reluctance to shame a boss, and the company could learn about problems before they became serious.

The lesson here: you have to keep focused on the overall business goal, but be open-minded so you can adapt to local environments.

## Merging & Acquiring Cultures, Not Just Businesses

We expect to find culture clashes when a business operates in different countries or regions, but the same kinds of clashes can occur when one company acquires another. Two companies may look complementary, compatible, and logically matched in terms of their products, services, and overall market positioning. But differences in how one organization's employees are used to working together and how they view the other organization can lead to an M&A culture clash as strong as any that occur between different countries or populations. The clash is often most evident in subtle or not-so-subtle actions that constitute uncivil behavior—and that's how M&As become an issue of civility. Left unaddressed, the differences can undermine the very purpose for which the deals were made.

Some of the lessons described above that deal with blending societal culture and business culture apply to M&A as well: the ultimate goal is to have one culture that is driven by common values that support business goals. Even when there is overlap or synergies between the acquiring and acquired companies, the cultures can be opposite in many ways. Perhaps one company is focused on fast-moving innovation and the other specializes in quality and control. Those two mentalities can often clash.

Blending cultures is hard work because typically you have long-standing, deeply rooted behaviors on all sides. So you have to articulate very clearly to the incoming organization what is acceptable and what isn't. To make sure the merger proceeds quickly and smoothly, the top leaders need to agree on what cultural norms will serve the combined entity best, and work to communicate those norms to people on all sides. Sometimes, this may mean educating one company on norms used in the other; or it may mean coming up with a combined model. Either way, you want all managers and executives to receive education and training within months of the merger so that employees across the whole organization will have shared expectations about behavior.

# Summary:
# A Meeting of Minds and Behaviors

When organizations have departments or divisions in different parts of the world, the cultural differences between work units are often obvious.

But the same kinds of culture clash can happen between people working down the hall or across the street from each other.

Part of leadership's role is to create a consistent internal culture no matter how dispersed the organization's work units are. Focus on the values and behaviors you want as internal standards as a way to achieve the best possible workplace, then look for ways to deliver on those standards while respecting local cultures.

# A Culture of Civility

**B**usiness people often toss around "culture change" like it's an insurmountable obstacle. True, it's extremely rare that there is a way to change culture that is quick, easy, *and* lasting, particularly when it involves the kind of entrenched, familiar behaviors written about here. But when people talk about the difficulties of changing and maintaining culture, I counter with a few examples of my own.

Here's one: For many years now, thousands of commuters in the Washington, D.C., area have slugged their way to work every day. Drivers go to various "slug lines" and pick up enough riders—they need three in a car—to use designated high-occupancy-vehicle (HOV) lanes that shorten commuting time.

It's common that drivers and riders don't know one another. Yet despite their unfamiliarity, everyone conforms to simple and clear principles of slugging etiquette. These rules are actually written down somewhere, but generally they are passed along by word of mouth. They govern a few essentials: who can say what, where riders are dropped, where people sit, whether the radio can be played (which is only if the driver wants it). Enforcement consists of a glare from a driver or a comment from another rider.

What I like about the slugging story is how clearly it demonstrates the easy way in which culture can be shaped:

- There are a few clear rules governing actions that matter to everyone involved.

- The rules are consistently enforced (and reinforced).

Because of this simplicity, the behaviors have been sustained for many years by many different people.

Most stories concerning culture change in business describe how complicated it is and how much time and investment it will take. Success will not be linear—there will be quick accomplishments, setbacks, even some stalls or reversals. I agree with all those statements, but I offer the slugging story as a way of demonstrating that if people share values and practices that have meaning to them individually and collectively, the behaviors consistent with those values will be self-enforced. If people recognize the importance of maintaining a particular culture in order to reap the rewards and there are immediate consequences if the norms are violated, establishing culture can be relatively easy.

There are many examples of behavioral norms that are enforced organically through culture rather than through formal programs. Anyone attending the Masters golf tournament knows not to bring in a cellphone or they will be tossed out. Fans attending sporting events know what colors they should and should not wear.

The same phenomenon holds true in most workplaces: clear but often unstated rules have a huge impact on the culture. A certain well-known consumer products firm doesn't allow anyone to bring in a product from their main competitor. The ancient rumor that is still passed from employee to employee is that doing so is grounds for dismissal (which supposedly happened once and now lives on as an apocryphal story).

# Envisioning a Different Future

As I've written this book over the past several years, I've thought about the future. How will organizations operate in ways that will leave legacies for future generations? It's clear that technology will increase and change our lives and work lives dramatically. No doubt there will be new ways to communicate, analyze information, and make decisions. There will be new jobs, new alliances; we'll have services that we could not currently imagine. The only sure prediction today is that 10 years, 20 years, 30 years into the future, the time in which we live right now will seem ancient, slow, and totally different.

I doubt, however, that we'll have difficulty recognizing the people issues of civility, inclusion, legality, and productivity that we deal with now and that have affected past generations. Saying that, I wonder about how Drs. Halsted and Cushing (discussed in Part 1) would practice medicine if somehow they were catapulted from their past into the future, our now. There is no doubt in my mind that they would bring with them two qualities: they would have the same intellect, technical skills, and brilliance that they had in their earlier lives and the same commitment to patient care and excellence—taken together, these are the core qualities of their professional lives.

When I read their biographies, I could almost feel the steel in their personalities when it came to doing the best for their patients. They would accept nothing less and were constantly looking for the most useful means of helping those under their treatment. That commitment to patient care explains why they worked so hard and were so passionate about the achievements for which they are known, ranging from the adoption of anesthesia and sterile practices to new procedures (in Halsted's case) or the development of neurosurgery (in Cushing's). Both recognized that what they did could save lives, and they directed part of their zeal to making sure that others understood and learned the impact of their particular causes.

Saying that, if they were alive now when medicine has changed so much (as have all of our professions), they would have read the articles and listened to experts linking outcomes and quality to teamwork and communication and been aware of instances where inappropriate, disruptive, unprofessional, and uncivil behavior led to catastrophic events. And my guess is they would have adopted the same passion for behavioral change, recognizing it as a core ingredient for excellence, as they would have to other discoveries, like the ones they had worked so hard to see widely adopted.

Focusing on civil treatment allows we leaders today to leave the kind of legacy that Halsted and Cushing would have left had they been educated about the importance of core values and the detrimental impact of uncivil behaviors. We can do that by recognizing the daily improvements we can make in terms of how we interact with each other and all employees, and the impact our behavior can have on present and future generations.

# Index

# ABOUT THE AUTHOR

**Stephen M. Paskoff,** Esq., is the founder, president, and CEO of ELI, a company that helps organizations solve problems, avoid risks, and improve business results through its Civil Treatment® learning program and consultation services.

Steve is a nationally recognized author and speaker on legal and behavioral issues in the workplace and how uncivil behaviors can limit productivity, creativity, and engagement. He has written extensively on topics related to workplace compliance, risks, and how to affect culture change in order to build lawful, professional operations that align with an organization's mission and values.

Prior to establishing ELI in 1986, Mr. Paskoff was a trial attorney with the Equal Employment Opportunity Commission and a partner in a management law firm. He is a graduate of Hamilton College and the University of Pittsburgh School of Law and is a member of the Pennsylvania and Georgia bars. He has been named the highest-ranking speaker at the national conference of the Society for Human Resource Management (SHRM) and has been a keynote speaker at a number of other national conferences.

In addition, Steve is a founder and current Co-Chair of the ABA's Compliance Training and Communication Subcommittee, which explores best practices in training methodology as well as overall strategies for implementing learning and communication plans to maintain corporate compliance. He has served on the Editorial Board of Workforce Management magazine and is a regular contributor to The Conference Board's Human Capital Exchange. He is the author of *Teaching Big Shots to Behave and Other Human Resource Challenges.*